Berlitz®

Corfu

D1102435

Berlitz Publishing Company, Inc.
Princeton Mexico City London Eschborn Singapore

Berlitz Trademark Reg. U.S. Patent Office and other countries
Marca Registrada

Text:	Paul Murphy
Editor:	Richard Wallis
Photography:	Paul Murphy except for pages 15, 18, 27, 41, 86, 96 by Donna Dailey
Cover Photo:	Donna Dailey
Photo Editor:	Naomi Zinn
Layout:	Media Content Marketing, Inc.
Cartography:	Raffaelle Degennaro

The author would like to thank Emma Catterall of Direct Greece.

*Although the publisher tries to insure the accuracy of all the infor-
mation in this book, changes are inevitable and errors may result.
The publisher cannot be responsible for any resulting loss, incon-
venience, or injury. If you find an error in this guide, please let the
editors know by writing to Berlitz Publishing Company, 400
Alexander Park, Princeton, NJ 08540-6306.*

ISBN 2-8315-7166-9

Revised 1999

Printed in Italy

040/104 RP

CORFU AND ITS PEOPLE

Swathed in a blanket of deep green, its mountainous sky-line plunging into a crystal-clear, turquoise sea, Corfu is known as Greece's Emerald Island. It is not only the greenest of Greece's myriad islands but one of the prettiest as well. Flowering bushes, shrubs, and trees cloak most of its rolling landscape, and in spring it is bursting with wildflowers.

Corfu's sunny beaches, spectacular scenery, and charming capital have enchanted visitors — including many writers and artists — throughout the centuries. The wonderful clear light and stunning vistas of the island are thought to have been the inspiration for settings in Homer's *Odyssey* and Shakespeare's *Tempest*. In more recent times, the British poet and painter Edward Lear depicted many views of Corfu's now famous sights, while the authors D. H. Lawrence and Gerald Durrell both lived here and wrote entertaining books about island life. Many past celebrities, from the Rothschilds to the Greek royal family and the empress of Austria, have had villas built on the island. This tradition continues today with many an Italian industrial magnate retreating to Corfu.

Over the last 20 years or so Corfu has become known as something of a British playground: Over half of all the island's holiday visitors come from the UK. No doubt early visitors felt very much at home sipping ginger beer and watching the cricket in Corfu Town — both relics of British rule (1814–1864) that can still be enjoyed today. The more recent introduction of cheap package-tourism in the 1970s and 1980s gave Corfu something of a reputation as a "party island." However, the party scene was always restricted to a few enclaves, and over the last few years some of those have mellowed considerably. Nonetheless, there are definitely still a few places that are best avoided by anyone who prefers the atmosphere of a Greek island to a rowdy British seaside town.

In keeping with island character and scale, many resorts are small, quiet, and secluded. Though development has been rapid on some parts of the island, it is still much less overbearing than in many other Mediterranean vacation destinations. In marked contrast to the European mainland, there are no high-rise horrors and only the occasional large hotel. Actually, much of the island remains untouched by mass tourism, and the main resorts are really crowded only in July and August.

The favored method of accommodation (particularly for those who know Corfu well) is the self-catering house or apartment. The island has scores — if not hundreds — of lovely villas and studios for rent. The best are often in the northeast corner, typically hidden away in dense green hillsides, just a couple of minutes walk from the nearest beach. Remarkably, even in peak season you can still find secluded places for sunbathing and hiking along the coastline and throughout the hilly hinterland. You just have to make that little bit of effort (usually either on foot or by boat) to get there.

> **Language is no problem for most visitors. Many locals speak English or Italian, and most signs are posted in both Greek and Latin characters.**

Corfu is the most northerly of the Ionian group of islands. Just across the water to the east are Albania and the Greek mainland. Only 74 km (46 miles) to the northwest is Italy. To the south are the delightful island of Paxos and the other Ionians (Levkas, Ithaca, Cephalonia, Zakinthos, and Kithera); island-hopping, however, is an option only for travelers with lots of time on their hands.

Corfu is also Greece's western gateway and has proudly styled itself "the entry to the Adriatic." It is no coincidence

Corfu is not a destination for island hopping, but picturesque Parga, on the mainland, is well worth a trip.

that the Turks — who conquered the rest of mainland Greece and its islands — failed to gain a foothold here. Instead, it was the great western European powers of the day (Venice, France, and Britain) who left their mark during 500 years of island occupation. Nowhere is this more noticeable than in the elegant architecture and cosmopolitan atmosphere of Corfu Town. Where else in the world could you sit at a French-style café, amid Venetian streets, sipping Greek coffee while watching English cricket? This stylish capital is regarded as the loveliest town in all the Greek islands, and a visit here is a highlight of most visitors' holidays.

In its shape Corfu resembles a scythe, measuring about 65 km (40 miles) in length and ranging in width from 4 km to 30 km (2.5 miles to 19 miles). According to geologists, the island is the exposed crown of a submerged mountain range that broke off eons ago from the mainland to the east. The highest point is Mount Pantokrátor, really only a fairly modest-sized peak of just over 900 m (2,950 ft). But on such a small island it takes on much more importance, and the summit is approached only by an impressive ascent along steep hairpin bends.

Hire a car, if only for a few days. No matter where you are based, you can very easily get around and explore the whole island. As you tour Corfu you'll see on the undulating hills

Sigá sigá **means "Slowly does it — take your time."**

and stone-hedged terraces silvery groves of prized olive trees — venerable, knotted, and gnarled. In the past they were an economic lifeline for the island, and they still provide excellent olive oil and wood for carving souvenirs. The island is also graced with legions of orange and lemon trees (giving off a glorious aroma), plane trees, jacaranda, palms, wisteria, myrtle, and oleander. Even the simplest homes are adorned with verdant grape arbors and enormous, beautiful clusters of roses or bougainvillea. Most memorable of all are the forests of tall, slim cypresses rising like sentries on the hillsides.

Visit in spring or early summer if possible to see the best of the island's flora: there are 100 native wildflowers alone that grow nowhere else. You might get a little wet then, but it's a price worth paying. The reason for Corfu's remarkably luxuriant vegetation is that more rain falls here — trapped by the nearby mainland mountains — than in any other part of Greece. For most of the year, however, this is very much an island in the sun.

Corfu has about 200 km (124 miles) of coastline with some of Europe's most beautiful — and cleanest — beaches. They vary from strips of pure golden sand to bright white pebbles and stones to combinations of all three. While swells for surfing can be found on the western shores, there are plenty of calm bays suitable for all the family on the more protected east coast. As for the sea itself, in any one cove the range of clear blues seems to defy the color spectrum. Don't miss a day-trip to Paxos, where the waters are Caribbean clear.

Just over 100,000 people live on Corfu. Some of them emigrate — attracted by life abroad or in the big mainland cities — but countless others have never left the island. Instead, the world comes to them, in increasing numbers that today reach 1 million annually. Yet despite the seasonal influx of visitors, the inhabitants on the whole retain a fresh, open simplicity that delights visitors.

Life on Corfu is cool, casual, and unhurried. For the punctilious northern European visitor it can sometimes be a bit too casual: waiting for the bus that is 20 minutes late (or never comes); the "fast-food" kebab for which you have to stand 15 minutes in line; the restaurant order that takes an eternity, then arrives cold! Be patient and just remember that nobody ever came to Corfu (or anywhere else in Greece, for that matter) for Swiss service, French food, or Scandinavian plumbing. After all, the slow pace of life here is the key to both *filoxénia* (the traditional Greek hospitality to strangers) and *filótimo* (local pride).

Corfu Town's cosmopolitan atmosphere and elegant architecture are a big draw.

HISTORY

Little is known about Corfu's first inhabitants. Prehistoric traces found at Gardiki in the southwest date back to the Paleolithic Era (70,000 B.C. to 40,000 B.C.), when the island was probably joined to the Greek mainland. But unlike on other Ionian islands, no traces of Mycenaean settlements have ever surfaced on Corfu, leading to speculation that the island might have been held by the Phoenicians for the course of that period (1500 B.C. to 1150 B.C.).

Corfu's acknowledged history begins in 734 B.C., when the Corinthians established a colony called Corcyra south of today's Corfu Town in an area known as Paleópolis (Old City). Archaeological digs (still in progress) have turned up evidence of temples near Kardáki Spring and Mon Repos, but the ancient city was otherwise destroyed by barbarian raiders, its stone blocks carried off to build medieval Corfu Town. The famous sixth-century B.C. Gorgon pediment from the Temple of Artemis, now in the Archaeological Museum, is the single most important surviving artifact of classical Corcyra.

Prospering from trade with southern Italy, Corcyra set up its own colonies on the nearby mainland and grew into a strong maritime power. In 665 B.C., Corcyra defeated Corinth in what the historian Thucydides noted as the first naval battle in Greek history. Thus did Corfu gain its independence from the mainland.

Corfu's pact with Athens against Corinth and Sparta in 433 B.C. proved to be, according to Thucydides, the final straw that set off the Peloponnesian War and brought about the end of classical Greece. From then on, Corfu suffered attack, pillage, and often highly destructive occupation. Situated just 74 km (46 miles) from Italy and only 2 km (1.2 miles) from the Albanian and Greek mainland at its nearest point, Corfu's safe harbors, fertile soil, and strategic position between the Adriatic and Ionian seas made it a prize worth contesting by the many powers fighting for control of the region.

Roman Conquest

Around 230 B.C. a Roman fleet arrived and took over control of the island, making Corfu the Roman Empire's earliest Adriatic conquest.

For the next five and a half centuries, Corfu prospered as a Roman naval base used for forays into the mainland. En route to and from battles — or simply as tourists — Nero, Tiberius, Cato, Cicero, Caesar, Octavian, and Mark Antony

Ulysses and the Stone Ship

According to Homer's *Odyssey*, the hero Ulysses ("Odysseus" in Greek) was shipwrecked during his ten-year voyage home from the Trojan War. He was washed ashore on the island of Schería — the ancient name of Corfu — which was inhabited by people known as Phaeacians. There he was found by Princess Nausicaa and her handmaidons when they came to wash clothes at a nearby stream. She persuaded her father, King Alcinous, to provide a boat to return him to his native Ithaca, but this assistance angered Poseidon (the god of the sea), who turned the ship to stone.

Three Corfu sites claim a starring role as the place described in Homer's epic poem where Ulysses' boat was petrified. All have the requisite double harbor approached by a narrow causeway as well as an offshore rock that (with a good dose of imagination) resembles a ship turned to stone. These are Mouse Island, off Kanóni; Kolóvri, off Paleokastrítsa; and Krávia (meaning "ship"), northwest of Cape Arílla. The beach where Ulysses was washed ashore is said to be the west coast's Ermónes, largely on account of its small stream.

(with Cleopatra) were among the Roman notables who visited Corfu. During the first century A.D., the two saints — Iáson (Jason) and Sosípatros — brought Christianity to the island. The ruins of Paleópolis, on the road to Kanóni, are among the few remnants from Corfu's Roman period.

The Byzantine Years

When the Roman Empire split in the fourth century A.D., its eastern half — Byzantium — took administrative control of Corfu but could provide little security. Rampaging Vandals raided the island in 445 and worse was to follow: In 562 a horde of Ostrogoths savagely destroyed Corfu's ancient capital and many monuments.

After foiling an attempted takeover by Slavs in 933, the Corfiotes moved their capital 2 km (1 mile) north and built their first fortress on the rocky bluff commanding the town's eastern sea approach. The Old Fort still stands today. Elsewhere, islanders abandoned coastal settlements and retreated inland to establish protected hillside villages.

Then appeared a formidable new enemy. Several times between 1080 and 1185 Norman forces crossed the Ionian Sea from Sicily to attack Corfu and nearby island outposts of the enfeebled Byzantine Empire. Out of desperation the rulers in Constantinople asked for help. The Venetians responded and thereafter took an active interest in the destiny of this Adriatic gateway island.

When Doge Enrico Dandolo and the crusaders conquered Constantinople in 1204, the spoils claimed by Venice included western Greece, parts of the Peloponnese, and the Ionian islands. But Venice was unable to extend immediate control over all its new holdings, and Corfu aligned itself with the Greek despotate (empire) of Epirus, which then controlled parts of what are today Albania and western Greece.

In 1214 Michaél Ángelos Comnenós II, head of the despotate, took control of the island, leaving as a legacy the fortresses of Angelokastro (high above Paleokastrítsa) and Gardíki (on the west coast). However, Sicily also had designs on Corfu. In 1259, to avoid all-out war, the island was presented to King Manfred, the Hohenstaufen king of Sicily, as his daughter's dowry.

Eight years later, the new king of Sicily and Naples, Charles d'Anjou, became the overlord of Corfu, where his family — the Angevins — subsequently ruled for over a century. During this time the traditional Eastern Orthodoxy of the island was almost extinguished by the new official religion of Roman Catholicism.

Venetian Rule

As the Angevin dynasty ended and its hold on the island diminished, Corfu's fledgling assembly of 24 barons, mind-

Ruins like these on the Albanian coast provide reminders of the various empires that have ruled the area.

Historical Landmarks

734 b.c.	Corinthians found colony of Corcyra.
665 b.c.	Corcyra defeats Corinth and gains independence.
229 b.c.–a.d. 337	Romans take control of Corfu, as their first outpost of their Empire in the Adriatic.
337–1081	Roman Empire splits; Corfu falls under control of Byzantine Empire.
562	Ostrogoths destroy ancient capital city and monuments.
933	Corfiotes move capital north and build first fortress.
1080–1185	Normans from Sicily repeatedly invade Corfu.
1204	Fall of Constantinople; Venice gains control of Corfu.
1214–1259	Epirus Empire takes control of Corfu.
1266–1386	Venetian occupation establishes Corfu as key port for commercial routes and important naval base.
1537	Corfiotes repel first Ottoman attack.
1571	Turks defeated in naval battle at Lepanto.
1716	Second Ottoman attack on Corfu repelled.
1797–1814	French control Corfu.
1814–1863	Corfu becomes a British protectorate.
1864	Corfu and Ionia ceded to Greece; British withdraw.
1916	Corfu gives refuge to exiled Serbian government.
1941–43	Italians and Nazis occupy Corfu during World War II; Corfu Town is badly damaged by German bombardment.
1944	Corfu liberated by the Allies.
1994	The island hosts European Union Summit.

ful of the danger presented by marauding corsairs, invited Venice to send in a protective military force. The Venetians landed on 20 May 1386, beginning an occupation that was to last without interruption for over four centuries. In the following year, Corfu officially became part of the Stato da Mar, the Venetian maritime empire.

Corfu prospered once again as a key port for galleys plying far-flung commercial routes. To strengthen the defenses of its vital harbor, the Venetians turned Corfu Town's old Byzantine fort into an impregnable bastion. It proved a wise move.

In 1463, having swept across mainland Greece, the Ottoman Turks declared war on Venice. During the following years they mounted many assaults on the Ionian Islands, and in 1537 they turned on Corfu. Intent on seizing Corfu Town, the Ottoman fleet — led by the Barbary pirate Khairel-Din (Barbarossa) — landed cannons and 25,000 troops north of the capital at Gouviá. The fortress withstood a bitter attack (which became legendary in Corfu history), but the rest of the island was looted and the vengeful Turks carried off some 15,000 to 20,000 prisoners — nearly half the population. Most of them were bound into slavery.

Following the great siege, the Venetians dug the Contrafossa, a canal separating the Old Fort from the town. They also erected a "New Fortress" (so-called even today) to guard the city's northwestern approach.

Corfu's finest military hour was to come in 1716, once more against the Turks and once more at great cost. After losing both Athens and the Peloponnese to the Venetians, the Ottoman sultan successfully counter-attacked, retaking some of the Ionian islands and sending 30,000 troops to quell Corfu.

Venice had hired foreign regiments under the German mercenary commander Johann Matthias von der Schulenburg to defend the island. For six bloody weeks the troops held out in

A dying Achilles outside the Achílleion Palace, built by Empress Elizabeth of Austria at the end of the 19th century.

Corfu Town. The Turks, with their overwhelmingly superior forces, ravaged the rest of the island. They appeared to be ready to capture the capital when they suddenly called off their assault and fled, apparently frightened away by a ferocious thunder-and-hail storm and — the populace devoutly believes — the intervention of St. Spyrídon bearing a flaming torch. In any case, the Turks did not return, and Corfu was the only part of Greece never to be subjugated by the Ottomans.

Throughout its long feudal occupation, Venice kept Corfu firmly in tow, a colony valued as an important naval base, trading depot, customs-collection station, and supply center. A civil-military governor and senior bureaucrats sent from Venice ran the island. Much like Venice's *Libro d'Oro,* a Golden Book listing the Corfiote nobility contained 277 families at the time that Corfu passed from Venetian hands to Napoleonic forces.

Ordinary islanders, however, were heavily taxed and denied public education. Nothing was done to restore the Greek Orthodox religion to its traditional dominance among the faithful people. Italian replaced Greek as the official language, even though the peasantry couldn't understand it and had no way of learning it. Many labored as serfs in the Venetian aristocrats' villas, some of which still dot the countryside.

More happily, Venice was responsible for nearly all the olive trees that grace Corfu's landscape. Eager to ensure a constant supply of oil, the republic at one stage decreed a cash bonus for every hundred trees planted. This new olive production permanently changed the island's economy for the better. An even more visible legacy is Corfu's old city: with its narrow streets and tall buildings, it is the most Venetian town in Greece.

Napoleon's Dream Island

In 1797 the republic of the doges fell to Napoleon, thus ending 411 years of Venetian occupation. For reasons that remain obscure, Napoleon was rather obsessed with Corfu. "The greatest misfortune which could befall me is the loss of Corfu," he wrote rather melodramatically to his foreign minister, Talleyrand. So, immediately after capturing Venice, Napoleon sent a force to occupy Corfu and the other Ionian Islands.

These French occupiers replaced Venice's autocratic rule with new democratic representation, burned Corfu Town's Golden Book, introduced public education, and made Greek the official language. Nevertheless, they still managed to antagonize the island's inhabitants by continuing to suppress the Orthodox Church. Within two years the French were driven out of the island by a joint Russo-Turkish force that reinstated Greek Orthodoxy as the official religion.

However, in 1807 the French regained Corfu from the Russians by the Treaty of Tilsit. This time Napoleon — never actually able to visit the island he'd called "the key to the Adriatic" — garrisoned the citadels with 50,000 men along with 500 new cannon, making Corfu one of the most powerfully fortified points in the eastern Mediterranean.

The French brought many other bonuses to Corfu. They established the first Ionian Academy for the promotion of arts and sciences, imported Greece's first printing presses, drew up a street plan for Corfu Town, built a miniature Rue de Rivoli (the Listón), and began the growing of potatoes and tomatoes, now mainstays of Corfiote cooking.

During this time the British carried on an ineffectual but irritating blockade of the island. They seized four neighboring islands from the French but had no hope of taking Corfu.

The British Move In

Napoleon's luck finally ran out. After his defeat at Waterloo, the British took Corfu in 1814. A year later, the Treaty of Vienna turned the seven Ionian Islands into one independent state under British protection. Corfu became the capital, and Sir Thomas Maitland was appointed the state's Lord High Commissioner.

The British occupation of Corfu lasted for just 50 years. While controversial, this protectorate brought certain benefits. Under Maitland, a road network was built. His successor had the road to Paleokastrítsa constructed and brought a permanent water-supply system to Corfu Town. While a number of changes were pure personal caprice on the part of the ten British High Commissioners, they also introduced new hospitals, model prisons, a decent judiciary, and religious freedom, ensuring the primacy of the Orthodox

Church. The slightly eccentric Lord Guilford — a philhellene who went about in classical Greek dress — established modern Greece's first university, the Ionian Academy, in Corfu Town in 1824. He bequeathed to it his library of 25,000 books and helped to make Corfu the country's chief literary and intellectual center of its day.

The constitution set in place by Maitland was another matter. Though maintaining a façade of parliamentary government with a Corfiote senate and assembly, the High Commissioner retained all power. Serious unrest first occurred in the 1820s, when Maitland stopped the Corfiotes from giving assistance to their

> The British left behind a number of stately buildings and monuments as well as cricket, ginger beer, and Christmas chutney — island favorites even today.

Greek mainland compatriots engaged in a war of independence against Turkey. This engendered widespread bitterness among the islanders.

As a strong movement for unification with the mainland arose after Greece gained independence in 1827, the British introduced token constitutional reforms (freeing the press and liberalizing election procedures), but the High Commissioner's power remained intact. However, nationalistic agitation for union — *énosis* — continued to grow, until even the most stubborn colonialist saw the writing on the wall.

Greek at Last

When the pro-British Prince William of Denmark became King George I at Athens in 1863, Corfu and the six other Ionian Islands were ceded to Greece as a gesture of goodwill to the new monarch. An agreement drawn up by the major powers of the day declared the islands "perpetually neutral," and, before hauling down the Union Jack, the British blew up the impressive for-

The church of Christ Pantokrátor dates back to the 16th century.

tifications they had added to Corfu Town. When they sailed off, the island's assembly made known its gratitude to Queen Victoria for this unprecedented voluntary withdrawal by a great power from an overseas possession.

Peace settled on the island in its early years as a province of Greece. Aristocratic tourists converged here, and Empress Elisabeth of Austria liked it so much that she commissioned an elaborate palace, which became the Achílleion.

Though officially neutral during World War I, Corfu effectively served as an Allied military and naval base, recalling the role the island had played in previous centuries. In 1916 Corfu gave refuge to the exiled government of Serbia and its troops after they were driven from the mainland. Thousands died from wounds and disease and now lie in the Serbian cemetery on Vídos Island.

In 1923 Mussolini gave an order for his fleet to bombard the island in reprisal for the alleged assassination of one of his generals on the Albanian-Greek border. Italian forces occupied Corfu briefly until they were obliged to withdraw under diplomatic pressure (primarily from Great Britain).

The Italians returned as occupiers in World War II. Mussolini issued new currency, and renamed streets, and signaled his intention to annex the Ionian Islands. However, Italy subsequently capitulated in 1943.

When the Germans tried to succeed their defeated allies, the Italian troops (who had now swapped sides) resisted on both Corfu and its sister island of Paxos. In the ensuing battle, nearly one-quarter of Corfu Town was destroyed, including the Ionian-style parliament house, the academy, and the municipal theater. After a year of occupation, German forces evacuated from Corfu in October 1944. The British moved in behind them, and peace descended once more.

Corfu was largely unaffected by the Greek civil war between communist and royalist partisans that raged on the mainland between 1947 and 1949. Since then, tourism and agriculture — the two economic mainstays of the island — have brought unprecedented prosperity to much of Corfu.

The First European

Corfu's most famous son is Ioánnis Kapodístrias (1776–1831). Born of a noble family, he became Greece's first president in 1827 and is hailed as the first statesman to envisage a unified Europe.

With the collapse of the Venetian Empire in 1797, Kapodístrias was instrumental in the creation of the Federation of Ionian Islands. He then served as a diplomat in the Russian court of Tsar Alexander. On a mission to Switzerland in 1813, he orchestrated the Swiss Federation, which has remained in place to this day.

In the ensuing years he began to develop ideas of a unified Europe in which no one member would become too powerful and in which the powers would collectively regulate the whole. In this vision he was a man ahead of his time. Sadly, his political ideals also brought him enemies, and he was assassinated on the Greek mainland in 1831. In 1994 his home island fittingly hosted a summit meeting of the very Union of which he had dreamed.

23

WHERE TO GO

Although Corfu Town is in many ways the heart and soul of the island, like most capitals it is neither typical nor representative. Unless you are traveling independently or just visiting Corfu on a whistle-stop tour, it is unlikely that you will be staying overnight in Corfu Town.

The vast majority of Corfu's visitors are on package tours and invariably stay on the coast at a broad range of accommodations — from cheap and cheerful hotels to luxury villas. Most such visitors are simply looking for "rest and recreation." Nonetheless, Corfu Town acts as a magnet for shoppers, culture vultures, or the merely curious, and it rarely disappoints. Located halfway down the east coast, it is within striking distance of any spot on the island. While hardly a convenient crossroads, it does makes a useful reference point for us to begin our island tour.

We divide our tour of the rest of the island into the following sections:

The South. The long, narrow southern portion of the island is often described (usually by people who haven't been to Corfu) as nothing more than a party zone. This is certainly true of its extremity (Kávos) but is not true when applied to the whole area. The Achílleion Palace is Corfu's most visited cultural attraction, while the long laid-back beaches of Ágios Geórgios and peaceful fishing villages such as Boukarí provide a sharp contrast to the busy resorts of Benítses, Moraḯtika, and Messongí, which are so popular with British visitors.

North of Corfu Town. Immediately north of the capital is the most developed part of the island. Its resorts are mostly hidden from the main road, occupying the large bays and inlets on this stretch of coastline.

The Northeast. Look in any brochure of expensive holiday villas and you will find most are set in the small area
between Barbáti and Kassiópi. The Durrells made Kalámi
the most famous resort on this stretch, but there are many
"Kalámis" nestling in the exquisite tiny coves that make this
area "connoisseurs' Corfu." A short distance inland looms
imperious Mount Pantokrátor.

Arriving in the Capital

If you are driving into Corfu Town, it's best to park as close
as possible to one or the other of the two forts; this helps you
get your bearings. The two forts effectively mark the town
center boundaries east and west. From the top of either one,
you can quickly appreciate the scale and layout below.

Driving in Corfu Town is less stressful than its myriad
streets would suggest, due to an efficient one-way system. If
you can't park by the Old Fort, you will simply be routed
round to the New Fortress.

Public buses set down either at San Rocco Square (blue
buses) or near the New Fortress (green buses). San Rocco
Square is Corfu's Piccadilly Circus or Times Square, intimi-
datingly busy at most times of the day. Despite being only a
stone's throw away from the tourist center of Corfu, this is a
very Greek, very foreign part of town, with most shops and
businesses catering to locals. Visitors who arrive by coach
excursion disembark close to the New Fortress and the
grassy gardens of the Esplanade.

Do note that our description of the town involves some
backtracking and — because things are so close together
— a little duplication. Corfu Town might be a relatively
small place, but it definitely rewards lingering. It is impossible to do the town justice in a single day. You should certainly aim to come here on Tuesday, Thursday, or Friday
evenings when the shops reopen.

The North and Northwest. While the north coast is well developed and dominated by the resorts of Sidári and Róda, the northwest is still something of a mystery to most visitors. The resorts of Ágios Geórgios and Ágios Stéfanos are very different from their namesakes south and east, respectively, Until recently they have been relatively isolated, but new roads are changing all that. The jewel of the northwest is Paleokastrítsa, boasting one of the most beautiful bays in all of Europe and retaining its charm despite its huge popularity.

The West. Between Ermónes and Ágios Górdis, the west is best for beautiful sandy beaches. Until recently it had escaped the attention of large-scale tourism, but development is now beginning to grow here as it has elsewhere on the island.

CORFU TOWN

Corfu Town is a beguiling place, with a relaxed, old-world elegance that rivals other Mediterranean cities many times its size. Its predominantly Venetian architecture is harmoniously flavored with French and English Georgian building styles, reflecting the influence of several centuries of foreign occupation. A cosmopolitan nature prevails, especially at night, when both Corfiotes and visitors stroll along the Listón and rendezvous at the many outdoor cafés and restaurants. In early August the atmosphere is very Italian.

Around the Esplanade

The focal point of Corfu Town is the **Esplanade** (Spianáda). Families promenade, marching bands parade, and festive occasions are frequently celebrated on this broad green expanse separating the Old Fort from the rest of town. The area was razed in Venetian times to give a clear field of fire against enemy assault, and it was also used for fairs and jousting tournaments. The French later planted the palms, eucalyptus trees, and flower gardens.

On the southern half of the Esplanade is the plain **Ionian Monument**, which celebrates the island's union with Greece in 1864. It is surrounded by marble reliefs displaying the symbols of the seven Ionian Islands, which are known as the "Eptanisa." Nearby is the Victorian bandstand (where Sunday concerts are held in summer) and the Maitland Rotunda, dedicated to the first British High Commissioner. At the far end is the statue of Greece's first president

Sir Frederick Adam, remembered as the creator of Corfu Town's aqueduct system.

(1827–1831) and Corfu's greatest son, Ioánnis Kapodístrias.

The Esplanade's most famous landmark is the cricket pitch dominating its northern half. Corfu adopted this sport during British rule, and enthusiastic local teams keep the tradition alive with matches during the season.

Across the north side of the Esplanade stands the imposing **Palace of St. Michael and St. George**, erected from 1818 to 1823 as the residence for the British High Commissioners, with a neoclassical façade of 32 Doric columns linking triumphal arches. It also housed the Ionian senate. When the British left, Greek royalty used it as a summer residence. The bronze toga-clad figure who stands above a lily pond in front of the palace is Sir Frederick

Adam, Britain's second High Commissioner. The pool and its water spouts are there to remind people that Adam was the first to ensure Corfu Town a reliable water supply, with an aqueduct system still in use today.

The palace's state rooms now house the **Museum of Asiatic Art**. Its collection of over 10,000 Asian artifacts is one of the most comprehensive collections of its kind in the world. Unfortunately, most of it has been closed to the public for some time; depending upon the degree of restoration, you might see only a tiny fraction of its wealth. Ancient pieces include funerary statuary and bowls, pottery, and ceramics from various Chinese dynasties and other Asian origins — Chou ritual bronzes, Ming Buddhas, ancient Cambodian stone heads, decorative dishware, intricate screens, armor, silks, and ivory.

That's Cricket

Corfu Town cricket pitch is one of the most unusual sportsgrounds in the world. Kim Hughes, the Australian captain during the early 1980s, once hit a mighty six right over the gardens and into the moat of the Old Fort here.

The mixed cultural heritage of the island can be heard in the cricketing language. "Play" is the Corfiote name for cricket. But, perhaps because of the long association with the Venetians, more than one term used during play has been lifted from Italian. So when a "long hop" becomes primo salto and cricket stumps are xyla ("wood" in Greek), the English might feel at a loss in their own game. Still, when the former England captain David Gower was asked where he had enjoyed playing the most, his immediate reply was "It has to be Corfu."

Matches generally take place on summer weekends starting at around 4pm or 5pm. Look in The Corfiote for details.

Around the back of the palace (on the Old Fort side), set in lovely gardens, is the lesser-known **Municipal Art Gallery**. It's a modest collection comprised of mostly 19th- and 20th-century works by Corfiote artists. Look for the *Assassination of Kapodistrias,* portraying the murder of the island's hero, as well as the charming, French-inspired *Night in Corfu,* which shows that even in 1913 the Listón was the place to be. After browsing the pictures, enjoy a coffee in the delightful setting of the adjacent art gallery café.

On the opposite side of the palace, just across the street, visit the pretty yellow building with an arcaded façade and an outside staircase leading up to a small loggia. It is home to the **Corfu Reading Society**, the oldest cultural institution in modern Greece, founded in 1836. Here on weekday mornings (closed in August), you can browse the history of the Ionian Islands in an archival collection of photographs, books, manuscripts, and other documents.

> Remember that the age-old tradition of the siesta is still alive and well among the Greek people. Local life simply stops for the afternoon.

The elegant arcades of the **Listón** border the west side of the Esplanade. Inspired by the Rue de Rivoli in Paris, it was built by the French in 1807. Its name comes from the "list" of noble families who were the only ones permitted to walk here. These days everyone gathers at the many cafés and bars under the arches or beneath the acacia trees along the green. During the evening this pedestrian-only street is transformed into a bustling promenade of Corfiotes and visitors alike, from dapper elderly men to smartly dressed families.

Stroll down the length of **Kapodistríou Street**, which runs from behind the Listón to the southern end of the green. It is lined with handsome homes, most of which were built by the

Inspired by the Rue de Rivoli, the Listón is a great place to take a stroll.

aristocracy, and several picturesque streets lead off here into town. Moustoksidi Street, for example, used to be an important thoroughfare and was also the setting for jousting displays during carnival, with the judges seated on the balcony above the ornate portico of the Ricchi mansion. At the very end of Kapodistríou, on Akadimias Street, is the pink façade of the old Ionian Academy, which was founded in 1824 by Lord Guilford as the first modern Greek university. Like much of the surrounding area, it has been completely rebuilt after suffering destruction in the heavy bombing of 1943.

Dousmáni Street cuts across the Esplanade to the Old Fort. Here you'll find a string of colorful 19th-century horse-cabs *(carrozzi),* which will take you on a ride around Corfu Town. Be sure to agree on the fare before you set out.

Old Fort

 Corfu Town grew up on the eastern peninsula around the **Old Fort**, which was erected for protection from barbarian raiders in the tenth century. The two peaks of the promonto-

Corfu Town Highlights

Archaeological Museum. *5 Vraíla Street; Tel. 0661 30680.* The gigantic, sixth-century B.C. Gorgon pediment from the Temple of Artemis and an archaic lion from the same period are the stars here. Open Tues–Sat 8:30am–3pm, Sun 9:30am–2:30pm. 800 drs.

Byzantine Museum. *off Arséniou Street; Tel. 0661 38313.* Beautiful icons and paintings from the 16th to 18th centuries, housed in a late-15th-century basilica. (There is also a small branch of the museum in the Old Fort.) Open Tues–Sun 9am–3pm. 800 drs.

Listón. *on the west side of the Esplanade.* Arcades built in 1807 on a French model. The many cafés and bars along the green are the site of one of Corfu Town's most elegant evening promenades and gathering spots.

Municipal Art Gallery. *Palace of St. Michael and St. George (no phone).* Worth a browse for the historical snapshots of old Corfu Town and the lovely café gardens. Open daily 9am–9pm. 500 drs.

Museum of Asiatic Art. *Palace of St. Michael and St. George; Tel. 0661 30443.* A remarkable collection from China, Japan, and other Asian cultures (though much of it might be closed). Open Tues–Sun 8:45am–3pm. 800 drs.

New Fortress. *entrance off Solomou Street; Tel. 0661 27447.* A small ceramics museum and great rooftop views of Corfu Town make the climb worthwhile. Open daily 9am–9pm. 800 drs.

Old Fort. *entrance off Esplanade; Tel. 0661 48310.* The small Byzantine museum, the fort's pretty boat-lined moat, and the best view of town — across the Esplanade — are the attractions here. Open daily 9am–9pm. 800 drs.

Paper Money Museum. *Ionian Bank of Corfu, 1st floor, St. Spyrídon Square; Tel. 0661 41552.* An extensive display of Greek banknotes and an impressive exhibit on how a banknote is designed and created. Open Mon–Fri 9am–1pm. Free.

ry on which it stands were the inspiration for the name Koryphó (*koryfí* means "summit" in Greek).

A statue of Count Schulenburg, the German mercenary who led the Corfiote defense against the Turkish attack of 1716, stands outside the entrance to the Old Fort, one of the many fortifications added by the Venetians to the older Byzantine citadel on the eastern peak. Its defensive moat, the Contrafossa, is lined with small boats and today makes for a very picturesque and peaceful scene. In turbulent times in the past, the bridge could be raised, cutting off all access to the fort.

The Venetian seat of government was here until it was destroyed by the British, who built barracks and a military hospital. The fort was then used by the Greek army until 1979. Restoration has been going on ever since, with the most recent additions being an excellent small Byzantine museum (admission included in the fort ticket) and a high-class shop specializing in museum replicas.

Once you are inside the fort complex, a path to the right leads to the garrison church of **St. George**, built by the British in 1840 as an Anglican chapel and restored after damage during World War II. Now converted to a Greek Orthodox church, it has a fine stone iconostasis and icons. Next door is a fashionable new café-restaurant.

Come back toward the entrance, where a stone path leads past a Venetian clocktower up to the lighthouse on the higher peak. The steep climb is well worth it for the spectacular panorama of Corfu Town, the harbor, the airport, and Mount Pantokrátor to the north.

From the Listón to the New Fortress

From the northern end of the Listón, walk along Kapodistríou Street, passing the Corfu Reading Society, and enter Arséniou Street. Look back to your right for a fine view of the Old Fort

The Byzantine Museum, in the Basilica of Antivouniótissa, contains an impressive collection of religious iconography.

and its marina. Immediately below is a small promontory, with a clutch of restaurants, cafés, and a swimming area.

The green, densely forested islet just offshore is **Vídos Island**, today a bird sanctuary but once the base for Ottoman attacks in 1537 and 1716. Its fortifications were destroyed when the British left the island in 1864, and it subsequently became a prison; the ruins are now a minor attraction. The island served as a refugee camp for around 150,000 Serbian soldiers during World War I. Sadly, some 30,000 of them died from influenza and other diseases caused by unsanitary living conditions; a mausoleum is dedicated to them. Boats regularly shuttle between the island and the Old Port.

A short way along Arséniou Street, a flight of steps leads to the excellent **Byzantine Museum**, housed in the 15th-century Basilica of Antivouniótissa (Church of the Holy

Virgin). The single-aisle, timber-roofed church is one of the oldest and richest on the island, constructed in the traditional Corfiote manner with a vestibule around three sides. In the museum there is an impressive array of icons from the 15th to 19th centuries.

Around the corner, the imposing profile of the **New Fortress** heaves into view. Below lies the Old Port, where you can catch ferries for Paxos (Paxí) and Igoumenítsa. The New Fortress (also known as the Fort of San Marco) was built by the Venetians in 1576, shortly after the second of two major Turkish sieges. You can see the Venetian emblem — the winged lion of St. Mark — in stone relief above the massive gates. The French, and later the British, completed the fortifications. The town's fruit and vegetable market is now held in the dry moat on the western side. A series of secret tunnels is said to connect the new and old fortresses (it is even said that there is a tunnel all the way across to Vídos Island!). At the top of the fort are a small, newly opened Ceramics Museum and an art gallery, but the finest sight is the superb view of Corfu Town and the far coast.

> The Greek word *Ágios* means "Saint." *Ágios Geórgios* is thus St. George. The plural ("Saints") is *Ágii.*

On the northern edge of Corfu Town's center — on the waterfront west of the New Fortress — is a lively nightlife strip with several clubs, bars, and good-time watering holes. These are particularly busy in the first half of August, when young Italian holidaymakers make merry.

The Commercial Center

The center of town starts roughly where G. Theotóki Street meets M. Theotóki Street (via Evagelistrias). Do note the first initials of these streets — there are several thorougfares

Relative terms — the New Fortress was built by the
Venetians in 1576, complete with a series of tunnels.

named after members of this long-established, illustrious
Corfiote family. Off M. Theotóki are five parallel shopping
streets, all of which run into Kapidistríou: Voulgareos, Ágios
Panton, Sevastianol, N. Theotóki, and Ágios Spyrídonos.

N. Theotóki is the commercial center's "High Street,"
leading all the way from the Old Port to Kapodistríou. Its
main square is Plateía Iroon (Heroes' Square); however,
because it backs onto St. Spyrídon's Church, it is better
known as Plateía Agiou Spyrídona (St. Spyrídon's Square.)
In the center of the square stands a statue of Corfiote politi
cian Geórgios Theotóki (1843–1916).

On the western side of the square stands the island's oldest bank, the Ionian, opened in 1839. It is home to the **Paper
Money Museum**, featuring an extensive display ranging
from early Ionian banknotes to world currency. More interesting than it sounds, this impressive collection illustrates all
the stages in designing, printing, and releasing notes for cir-
culation. Adding to the confusion, the bank has given the
square yet another unofficial name: Plateía Ionikí.

Across from the bank stands the **Faneroméni** church, also
called Our Lady of the Strangers (Panagía Ton Xénon)

because it was occupied by refugees from the mainland during the time of the Turkish occupation of Greece. Erected in 1689, it is lavishly decorated with gilded wood, a beautifully painted ceiling, and icons by Cretan painters. Opposite is a simpler church, **St. John the Baptist** (Ágios Ioánnis o Pródromos). Built in 1520, it was formerly Corfu's cathedral and also contains important Cretan paintings.

The red-domed bell-tower of the church of **Ágios Spyrídon**, the tallest on the island, rises north of the square. It was built in 1590 to house the mummified body of Corfu's beloved saint, who lies in an ornate silver coffin in a chapel

St. Spyrídon

Corfiotes pray to him, swear by him, name their sons after him, and honor him with a remarkable passion. He is the island's beloved patron saint, yet he wasn't even born on Corfu.

Spyrídon was a village shepherd on the distant island of Cyprus. He became a monk, then a bishop, and was noted for his devoutness and ability to effect minor miracles. After his death in A.D. 350, a sweet odor wafted from his grave; his body was exhumed and found to be perfectly preserved. The saint's remains were taken to Constantinople but were smuggled out (with those of St. Theodóra Augusta) before the Turkish occupation in 1453. Unceremoniously wrapped in a sack of straw strapped to a mule, the remains arrived in Corfu in 1456. In time, Spyrídon became the object of enthusiastic veneration.

To honor his miracles, his casket is paraded through Corfu Town in colorful processions on Orthodox Palm Sunday, Easter Saturday, 11 August, and the first Sunday in November. St. Spyrídon has reputedly saved the island four times: twice from the plague, once from famine, and once (in 1716) from the Turks. Small wonder that most Corfu men are named Spíros.

to the right of the altar. On certain days the casket is opened, and on special feast days the saint is paraded upright through town. His shrunken face can be seen through a glass panel and his slippered feet are exposed for the faithful to kiss. With all the rich Venetian oil lamps swinging above the casket (plus the chandeliers and the candelabra), this modest, dimly lit church is said to have the greatest amount of silver of any Greek church outside the island of Tínos. Paintings on the ceiling depict the saint's miracles.

Leave the church by the front entrance, on Spiridonos Street. Go to the left to meet Filarmonikis Street. Here you can turn right to explore the Old Town. Or you can turn left to reach M. Theotóki Street to see more of the shopping district. (If you have time do both, see the Old Town first and then retrace your steps).

Follow M. Theotóki Street to the corner of Voulgáreos Street, behind which is **Plateía N. Theotóki**, once the main square of the old town. It too has another name: Plateía Demarchíou (Town Hall Square). At the lowest part of the square sits the **Town Hall**, one of Corfu's most decorative buildings. Built by the Venetians in 1663 out of white marble from the eastern slopes of Mount Pantokrátor, its original single-story loggia served as a meeting place for the nobility. It was converted into a theater in 1720, and later a second story was added. It became the Town Hall in 1903. The façade is adorned with carved masks and medallions. On the eastern wall there is a bust of Francesco Morosini, the Venetian commander who defeated the Turks at Athens in 1687.

Handsome steps and flower-decked terraces ascend above the square, past restaurants and some smart shops. The stately building at the top was originally the Catholic archbishop's palace. It was subsequently converted into the Law Courts, and now it is home to the Bank of Greece.

The charming 17th-century Town Hall Square was the center of administration in Venetian times.

☞ The Old Town

The **Old Town** (or Campiello) is the fascinating maze of narrow streets, steep stairways, and arched alleys squeezed into the northeast quadrant of Corfu Town, between the Old Fort and the Old Port. It has been described as Greece's largest "living medieval town." As you wander along the flagstone streets, peeking into open houses, you might feel that this traffic-free, tall-walled quarter is like a miniature Venice — minus the canals, of course!

In Venetian times, the area between the old and new forts was surrounded by city walls (torn down during the 19th century). As Corfiotes weren't permitted to live outside the walls, the only direction in which they could expand their living quarters was upward, producing the district's unusually high buildings. And, just as in the less touristy parts of Venice, much of the Old Town's appeal is in its residential atmosphere, with laundry strung across alleyways, old women on stools weaving or keeping an eye on babies, and cats snoozing in tiny sun-splashed squares. The only "sight" is the charming 17th-century **Venetian Well** in Plateía Kremastí, where one of the city's best restaurants sets out its tables.

There are many ways of entering the Campiello, and it's a good place to simply wander at will. However, here is one way to find the Venetian Well from the landmark church of St. Spyrídon: outside the church (front entrance), turn left into Ágios Spyrídonos Street and, at the end, turn right into Filarmonikis, then left again into Filellínon, a narrow passageway lined with shops. The maze-like streets that make up the heart of the Campiello will be to your right. As you emerge from Filellínon, turn right into Ágios Theódoras. Look for a short flight of steps on the left, which lead to Plateía Kremastí.

By retracing your route along Ágios Theódoros, you'll reach Corfu's **Orthodox Cathedral**, built in 1577 and dedicated to St. Theodóra, the island's second-most revered saint (after Spyrídon). Her headless body, which was spirited out of Constantinople (along with Spyrídon's), lies in a silver reliquary to the right of the altar screen. There is a serene, slightly Eastern beauty to this small church. Broad flights of steps lead down to the harbor, and Corfiotes often momentarily pause here to light a candle before or after a sea journey.

Archaeological Treasures

The island's prime collection of antiquities is a five-minute walk south of the Old Fort, along the coastal road past the marina. A signpost announces the **Archaeological Museum** just after the Corfu Palace Hotel.

This pleasantly airy, modern museum houses two of the finest works of antiquity ever found. The star attraction, the **Gorgon pediment**, comes from a Temple of Artemis (sixth-century B.C.) at ancient Corcyra. It derives its name from the ferocious, sculpted Medusa (the most infamous of the three snake-haired gorgons), shown here with wings at her back, winged sandals, and serpents at her waist. She is flanked by her offspring, born from her dying blood: Pegasus, the winged horse, and the hero Chrysáor. Beside her stand two alert lion-panthers waiting to obey the commands of this monster who, according to the myth, turned anyone who met her gaze to stone. The pediment was discovered in 1912 at Paleópolis and is Greece's oldest existing monumental sculpture. What makes it particularly fearsome are the glazed, bulging eyes and the sheer scale: She stands some 3 m (10 ft) tall.

> If you are given a candle when entering a church, light it from another burning candle and place it with the rest. Then place a donation in the offerings box.

Not so colossal — but almost as important in archaeological terms — is the archaic lion in the adjoining room. This remarkable sculpture, dating from the same period as the Gorgon pediment, was found near the Tomb of Menecrates in 1843 and is thought to have graced the grave of a warrior during Corfu's struggle for independence from Corinth. The lion was chiseled by an unknown Corinthian artist and is considered one of the most beautiful ancient animal sculptures.

Among the museum's other treasures, which include pottery, coins, bronze statuettes, figurines, and Neolithic artifacts, is the series of small statues depicting the goddess Artemis in her different guises as huntress, protector, and guardian of the hearth. They are thought to have been produced for local worshippers in what might have been Corfu's first souvenir shop.

A five-minute walk south of the museum brings you to another treat for archaeology enthusiasts. The **Tomb of Menecrates** lies one block inland from the monument to Sir Howard Douglas, another High Commissioner, at the intersection of the coastal road and Alexandras Avenue. This circular stone cenotaph with a conical roof was a tribute to Menecrates, a mercenary who fought on the mainland in Corcyra's interests. It dates from about 600 B.C.

The Villa of Mon Repos is not open to the public, but its leafy surrounding grounds are.

As you head back toward the center of town along Marasli Street, it is a five-minute walk to the serenely beautiful **British Cemetery**, which retains special significance for a large number of British and Commonwealth visitors. Among the tall cypress trees and meticulously kept flowers and shrubbery (beautiful wildflowers, even orchids, also grow here) lie graves that date back to the start of Britain's protectorate. There are graves of British servicemen from the two World Wars as well. The circular wall south of the cemetery encloses the penitentiary. Built by the British, it was once the most modern penal institute in Europe, with individual cells for inmates. It is still in use today.

Corfu Town's Southern Suburbs

To explore this part of Corfu you will need transport. Head south along the coastal road for about 2 km (a mile or so) and turn inland (right) to the Byzantine **Church of Ágii Iáson and Sosípatros**. Built of limestone, brick, and tile, this is one of only two surviving Byzantine churches on the island. It is dedicated to Saints Jason and Sosípatros, the militants credited with bringing Christianity to Corfu in the second century. The present church dates back to the 12th century, though earlier versions stood here during Corfu's Byzantine period (337–1204). The black marble columns in the vestibule and a number of the large blocks used for the walls are thought to be from Classical buildings. The church has been undergoing major renovation work.

Farther along the road to Kanóni stands the entrance to the villa and gardens of **Mon Repos**. Built in 1831 by High

Soak in the beauty of the quaint islets and coastal scenery surrounding Kanóni.

Commissioner Frederick Adam as a summer residence, it later became the property of the Greek royal family. (Prince Philip, the duke of Edinburgh, was born here in 1921.) In recent years Mon Repos was the subject of an ownership dispute between the ex-king, Constantine, and the government, and this was only recently resolved. However, the estate might not be signposted, and many would-be visitors simply drive straight past. Watch for a large arch with a blue E.U. sign and a small parking area on the opposite side of the road facing a huge ruined church.

The villa of Mon Repos is not open to the public, but its extensive grounds are. Paths go up to the house itself, which will in the future probably hold museum displays dedicated to Paleópolis (see below). The paths also wind along the wooded promontory, past an old chapel with vine-covered arbors, up to a scenic view of the shore below. Follow the "ancient temple" signs to the remains of a small Doric temple, which dates from around 500 B.C.

The Ancient City

Opposite the Mon Repos gate lie the commanding ruins of **Agía Kérkyra**, or Paleópolis Church. The fifth-century basilica is the oldest church on the island, constructed from remnants of far older pagan temples that once stood on the site. It was ruined by invaders, rebuilt several times in the ensuing centuries, then destroyed again in World War II.

In the eighth century B.C., the original Corinthian city of Corcyra sprawled over much of this area, now called **Paleópolis**. You'll see archaeological digs in progress (no entry). The side of the dig site opposite the basilica leads to the hamlet of Análypsis, thought to be the acropolis of the ancient city of Corcyra. From the church at the top of the hill there is a superb view of the Mon Repos grounds.

Near the roundabout at Análypsis, a steep path leads down to **Kardáki Spring**. The water that flows from the mouth of a stone lion — cool in the summer and warm in the winter — is reputed never to dry up. Legend has it that anyone who drinks from the spring is destined to return to Corfu.

Along the road toward Kanóni, you'll see a side road marked "Stratia." Here are the ruins of the **Temple of Artemis**, where the gorgon in the Archaeological Museum was excavated. Next door is the Convent of Ágios Theódoras. Farther along the road stands one of the sections of the wall of ancient Corcyra, dating from the fifth century B.C.

Kanóni

Generations of earlier visitors once knew **Kanóni** as a tranquil green peninsula, a pleasant walk or carriage ride south of the capital. Popular with Corfiotes, it also used to attract large groups of British residents, who came to admire the most famous view on the island: the two islets resting peacefully in the Chalikiópoulos lagoon.

Times have changed. New hotels and blocks of flats have disfigured the landscape. The motivation for building hotels and residences here is unclear, as many of their views are of the shallow and murky lagoon and the adjacent international airport runway, complete with thunderous sound effects. In fact, it might be said that Kanóni has come full circle: its name derives from the gun battery that the French installed on the hillside here in 1798.

Nevertheless, the delightful picture-postcard **view** of the islets and the coastal scenery beyond them remains intact, attracting an endless stream of tour buses to Kanóni. A far nicer way to arrive is on the boats that run hourly from Corfu Town.

Contrary to popular belief, the islet in the foreground — linked to the mainland by a causeway — is not Mouse Island

The Achílleion Palace, among Corfu's most popular attractions for visitors, has its share of detractors, too.

but **Vlachérna**, which is home to a pretty, tiny white convent. **Mouse Island** (or Pondikoníssi) lies a three-minute boat trip away. There, an even smaller 13th-century chapel lies hidden beneath the cypress trees, though in reality it is of little interest and is hardly worth the journey. Mouse Island is another contender for the site of the mythical Phaeacian ship turned to stone (see page 122).

A pair of café-restaurants on the hill provide a relaxing terrace from which to enjoy the magnificent view. A pedestrian causeway below leads across the lagoon to Pérama. If you are an adrenaline junkie, you might well enjoy standing on this causeway as a plane takes off just a few feet above your head.

The Achílleion Palace

Described by the British writer Lawrence Durrell as "a monstrous building" and by the American Henry Miller as "the worst piece of gimcrackery," the **Achílleion Palace** is one of the most popular sights on the island (and usually teeming with tour coaches). Some 10 km (6 miles) south of Corfu Town, the palace's most recent claim to fame is as a backdrop in the James Bond film *For Your Eyes Only* — giving even more sarcastic ammunition to its detractors.

A romantic past as an imperial hideaway is a large part of the attraction. The beautiful Empress Elisabeth of Austria (familiarly known as Princess Sissy) fell in love with this site on a visit to the island during the 1860s. Thirty years later —

> *Endáxi* is colloquial for "Fine" or "Okay."

desperately unhappy, stifled by the pomp of Vienna, and stricken by the death of her only son — she looked back with longing to Corfu. In 1890 she purchased this land and commissioned the building of a palace that would be worthy of her idol, the Greek hero Achilles. The result, built in the neoclassical style of the late 19th century, was widely criticized as being tasteless and ostentatious.

The empress nonetheless spent as much time as she possibly could at the Achílleion, in utmost seclusion in the spring and autumn of each year. But poor Sissy had only a few years to enjoy her palace. Her tragic life came to a premature end in 1898 when, during a visit to Switzerland, she was mortally stabbed by an Italian anarchist.

In 1907 Kaiser Wilhelm II of Germany acquired the palace, deeming it a suitable base from which to pursue his archaeological hobby. He invited dignitaries from all over Europe to attend parties and concerts here. Because most arrived by boat, he built a special bridge at the seashore that crossed the coastal road directly to his palace. The ruins of the bridge remain today. The Kaiser also installed an awesome 4.5-ton bronze *Victorious Achilles,* which looms some 11.5 m (38 ft) high at the far end of the gardens.

The Achílleion was used as a military hospital in World War I. It subsequently became property of the Greek government, and from 1962 to 1983 its opulent upper floors were converted into a casino. In the 1990s, after renovation and the removal of its casino, the palace was opened to the public. Note. The first floor is not accessible to visitors.

The Achílleion is adorned both inside and out with a flurry of pseudo-classical statues, with Greek gods, goddesses, and heroes filling every corner. Those surrounding the Peristyle of the Muses, outside the palace, are copies of the ones in Rome's Villa Borghese gardens. Do make sure to peer through the window here to see the giant painting *The Triumph of Achilles* by Franz Matz. (You will find it on the first floor of the palace, which is closed to the public.) Our hero is shown in brutal, vengeful form dragging the body of Hector behind his chariot around the walls of Troy as a reprisal for the killing of Achilles' friend Patroclus.

Always ask permission before you take a picture of people. Some older folks do not like it.

Among all the statues scattered about the grounds, only one is considered by experts to have any artistic merit: the dramatic *Dying Achilles,* by German sculptor Ernst Herter.

Inside, the ground-floor rooms house a small chapel and the original furnishings and memorabilia of the empress and the kaiser. One unusual attraction is the adjustable saddle on which Wilhelm used to sit while writing at his desk.

The extensive grounds are perhaps the true highlight of the Achílleion. The manicured hilltop gardens are a real pleasure, with magnificent sweeping views over the island.

THE SOUTH

Benítses, some 12 km (7.5 miles) south of the capital, used to be the island's nonstop party town. It is now a victim of its own excess. Several tour operators pulled out of the resort, and over the last few years the party has almost come to a complete stop.

Arriving from the north, the first thing you will see in Benítses is the **Shell Museum**. This impressive exhibition of seashells, corals, fossils, starfish, and sponges was collected throughout the world by a Corfiote. It is one of the best private shell collections in Europe. The many specimens on display range from huge clamshells to tiny delicate cowries, fearsome shark's jaws, spiny crustacean skeletons, and stuffed pufferfish.

It is thought that Benítses might have been a holiday center as far back as the time of the Romans. Behind the harbor square stand the meager remains of what was once a Roman bathhouse, together with some floor mosaics. This northern end of town, near the old harbor, has a very Greek atmosphere, with

A beack by any other name — San Barbara, Ayia Várvara, Marathia, or Maltas. Its beauty remains the same.

pretty cottages that retain the character of the original fishing village. The emerald valley at the western edge of town is criss-crossed with footpaths in an unexpected wilderness.

The busy coastal road continues south as far as the twin resorts of Moraítika and Messongí, 20 km (12.5 miles) from Corfu Town. They lie at the mouth of — and are divided by — the Messongí River. This is an attractive spot, with fishing and pleasure boats moored alongside the riverfront.

Moraítika is the busier and livelier of the two villages. Its older section is set on a hill just off the main road and marked by a red-and-yellow campanile. There is no tourist development up here, just an attractive taverna or two providing a nice antidote to the seaside resort below. Like Moraítika, **Messongí** features an increasing amount of development now spreading back from the long but very narrow beaches. Behind the beach, Messongí boasts some of Corfu's oldest olive groves, planted by Venetians over 500 years ago. The hills are perfect for walking.

From here the main road south curves inland and reaches a T-junction at Ano Messongí. The route north takes you inland through the pastoral scenery of the Messongí River valley before ascending the slopes of Corfu's second tallest mountain, the 576-m (1,889-ft) Ágii Déka ("Ten Saints"). From **Ágii Déka** village there is a spectacular view out to sea, overlooking Benítses and the far Kanóni peninsula.

An alternative route to the southern tip of the island is not to turn inland but to follow the minor road that runs along the coast southward from Messongí. Along this peaceful, tree-shaded shore are small seafood tavernas and narrow, pebbly beaches where you can soak up the tranquil bay view. It's a far cry from the busy international resorts you have just passed. This pretty stretch of coast ends at the small fishing village of **Boukári**. But if you would like a little more of the same, try another detour, either to the little fishing village of Nótos or to Petriti, another quiet spot where fresh fish is a specialty.

Directly opposite here, on the other (western) side of the coast, lies Ágios Geórgios, the island's longest sandy beach, nicknamed "Golden Sands." To get to the west coast, return to the main road where the old monastery at Argirádes sports a striking Venetian belfry. Head south for 2 km (1.2 miles), and at Marathia a makeshift sign points down to the right, to "the beach." This refers to a beach known by several names: **San Barbara**, Ayia Várvara, Marathia, or Maltas. Whatever the name, it is an attractive broad beach of soft golden sand at the southern extremity of Ágios Geórgios. Development is small-scale and spreads out without any real focus.

To get to **Ágios Geórgios** itself, you must head back north and then turn left shortly after Argirádes. The turnoff takes you to the busiest part of the beach, although development is still relatively light in this fledgling resort area. The beach is

The Venerable Olive

Almost everyone on Corfu owns a few olive trees. In Venetian times, peasants were paid for each tree they planted, and by the 17th century a family's wealth was determined by the number of trees it owned. Today there are said to be 3.5 million on the island.

According to legend, St. Spyrídon appeared in an olive grove and proclaimed that cutting or beating the trees was cruel. As a result, Corfiotes neither prune the branches nor pick the fruit. Instead, they let the olives fall to the ground naturally, where huge nets are spread to catch them. Trees bear fruit only every other year and might take 12 years to yield a first crop.

Highlights Around the Island

Opening hours are for the high-summer season; hours might be reduced during other periods.

Achílleion Palace. *Gastoúri; Tel. 0661 56210*. The island's most controversial and bombastic building, in a lovely garden setting. Open daily 8am–7pm. 1000 drs.

Angelókastro. *Krini, near Paleokastrítsa (no phone)*. Some of the island's best views can be enjoyed from the summit of this ruined Byzantine castle. Open daily at any time (might be closed for restoration work). Free.

Castello Art Gallery. *Castelino at Káto Korakiána, near the resort of Dassiá; Tel. 0661 93333*. This department of the Greek National Art Gallery offers changing exhibitions. Open daily 10am–2pm and 6pm–9pm in summer; daily 10am–1pm in winter. Free.

History and Folklore Museum of Central Corfu. *Sinarádes; Tel. 0663 38193*. An authentic look at Corfiote life from the last century. Open Mon–Sat 9:30am–2pm. 350 drs.

Kalámi and Kouloúra Bays. The most famous bays on the northeast coast, with picture-postcard beaches.

Myrtiótissa Beach. Corfu's softest sand on its most picturesque stretch of beach, located on the west coast. A bit of a trek to get there, but well worth the effort.

Paleokastrítsa Monastery. *Paleokastrítsa (no phone)*. Escape the crowds by visiting this peaceful little gem at the end of the day. Open daily 7am–1pm and 3pm–8pm. Free

Pantokrátor Monastery and **Mount Pantokrátor**. Situated at the island's highest point, this peaceful monastery church is an ideal place for quiet reflection. The scenery along the steep and winding route to the top of the island is every bit as enjoyable as the views from the summit. Open 1 April–31 October only: 7am–12:30pm and 2:30pm–8pm (often open all day in summer). Free.

very attractive, with gold sand backed by cliffs that rise and fall. With such a long stretch of inviting coast, you can always find your own patch of sand.

The northernmost part of the beach is Issos, which borders **Lake Korissíon**. To get there you have to return to the main road, head north, and turn left at Linia. Lake Korissíon is used as a fish farm and is thus off-limits for swimming or boating, but birdwatchers will find plenty to observe here, particularly in spring and autumn. The scenery is quite wild, with tall dunes providing shelter for nudists and large wind-carved rocks giving a lunar-like landscape. This was a setting for a chase scene in the James Bond film *For Your Eyes Only*. Windsurfing conditions here are excellent.

There is little of interest south of the San Barbara beach turnoff. This is olive, orchard, and vegetable country as well as the island's principal wine-producing region. **Lefkímmi** is the hub of this working agricultural region, bypassed by a very fast roadway that goes all the way to the southern tip of the island.

Kávos is the end of the road, the last resort — in just about every respect. To Corfiotes, the very name brings a shake of the head and a "tsk tsk" of disapproval. Development has mush-roomed in recent years, with a profusion of apartments, hotels, and scores of nightspots and music bars flourishing incongru-ously on this remote tip of the island. Young booze-fueled rev-elers flock here in July and August, earning a (well-deserved) reputation for being the rowdiest on the island. That said, the soft sandy beach that extends for 3 km (nearly 2 miles) is very shallow; it's popular with families earlier in the season.

There's a variety of watersports available here, as well as di-rect boat excursions to Paxos, Antipaxos, and Párga as well as to Sivota (on the Greek mainland). A walk through peaceful countryside leads to Cape Asprókavos, the island's southern-most tip, and the derelict monastery of Panagía Arkoudíllas.

NORTH OF CORFU TOWN

The former fishing villages north of Corfu Town are now home
to some of the island's liveliest and most popular resorts.

The villages of Kondokáli and Gouviá lie within a shel-
tered lagoon about 8 km (5 miles) north of Corfu Town. They
are set back from the busy main highway and linked by a
small road, with side tracks leading to sand and pebble beaches and a large marina.

Gouviá, named after the bay on which it stands, is the
more developed of the two villages, with a narrow, compacted sand beach dominated by large hotels. One section
is even fronted with concrete so that the sea (shallow and
still at this point) looks more like a municipal boating
pond than the Ionian. Across the pretty bay you can see the
little church of Ipapandí (Michaelmas), which juts out on
a stone spit rather like the famous "Mouse Island" vista.

*Watersports — both easy and extreme — are a way of life
for many Corfiotes and visitors to the island.*

Beyond is the island of Lazaretto, which formerly housed a quarantine station.

The extensive harbor of Kondokáli has become a private international marina lined with expensive yachts. It was once a Venetian naval base, and the skeletal arches of an old Venetian arsenal and shipyard survive at the end of Gouviá's beach. It's a long way round to get to the marina entrance, and its gate is manned by a guard who will ask your business.

The resort of **Dassiá** ("forest") is backed by dense olive groves lying between the main road and the sea. There is no central village, just a long string of restaurants, shops,

> Try not to waste water: it's a precious commodity all over Greece. But when the cicadas stop chirping — beware! It heralds rain.

and bars along a very busy main road. The beach, however, is tucked away down side roads. It is long and narrow, made up of compacted sand and pebbles, and it is often crowded. There are numerous clubs providing water skiing, jet skiing, and parasailing from the long piers jutting out into the bay. The continual stream of colorful parachutes launching off jetties against the blue sky — with the verdant olive groves and mountains in the background — is a fine sight.

To escape the hustle and bustle, wander inland on an uphill journey past quiet villas and olive groves to **Káto Korakiána**. Here, set in the grounds of an old Venetian villa (the Castello Mansion), is the **Castello Art Gallery**, which exhibits works on loan from the Greek National Art Gallery.

The twin resorts of **Ípsos** and **Pyrgí** are situated on a wide, beautiful bay about 15 km (9.5 miles) north of Corfu Town. Together they have been dubbed "the Golden Mile" by the armies of young, largely British singles who tend to congregate in the pandemonious discos and bars of this area during the high season. The long, narrow beach that curves around the bay is a mixture of sand and shingle and offers an excellent selection of watersports facilities. The main road runs immediately parallel to the beach, however, so this is not a spot for peace and quiet.

In times past, Ípsos Bay was a target for Turkish raiders. It is said that the name *Ípsos,* meaning "heights," was a ruse to dissuade the Turks from mounting an attack. *Pyrgí,* meaning "tower," probably derives from watchtowers built to warn of imminent raids.

The resorts themselves are recent creations, developing around resettlements of villagers from Ágios Márkos whose homes were destroyed in landslides during the 1950s. Ípsos at least has retained its fishing fleet, tucked away in an attractive little harbor behind the road as you enter from the south.

The tranquil old village of **Ágios Márkos** (St. Mark), signposted just outside Pyrgí, is worth a detour for its glorious views of the coastline and its two churches. At the top of the village is the 16th-century church of Christ Pantokrátor, with fresco-covered walls. Lower down, the 11th-century Ágios Merkoúrios, also with ancient frescoes, is Corfu's oldest Byzantine church (the only other one to be found on the island is the church of Ágii Iáson and Sosípatros, in Corfu Town). Both churches are kept locked, but ask in the bar on the main road and the keyholder might be found for you.

Mount Pantokrátor

Just beyond the Ágios Márkos turnoff, a road leads to the summit of **Mount Pantokrátor** (900 m/2,950 ft). Around a series of corkscrew bends you'll be greeted by stupendous views over Ípsos Bay. Just below the colorful village

of Spartílas, the road broadens out into a rolling landscape of fruit trees, fields, and vineyards where some of Corfu's finest wine is produced. At Strinílas there is an inviting bar and café beneath a large elm tree. From this point, continue following the signs to Mount Pantokrátor.

In the past the summit could be reached only by hiking along a somewhat treacherous gravel track. Today you can drive all the way to the top, but be forewarned that parking space at the summit is limited. If it is busy, park and walk up the last hundred meters. On a clear day you will be rewarded with unbeatable views: the entire sickle outline of Corfu and, over the narrow channel, a glimpse of Albania. To the south, in the blue Ionian, lie the islands of Paxos and distant Cephalonia.

Kouloúra is one of the most beautiful — and visited — locales on the island.

The mountaintop monastery, which shares the summit with an ugly aerial complex, was constructed during the 17th century on the site of an earlier church that had been built by neighboring villagers in 1347. It has been restored in recent years and is a charming, dark, and peaceful haven with many ancient frescoes and icons.

It is also possible to get to the top of Mount Pantokrátor from the northeastern part of the island (see page 61). A good tour choice is to go up one side and come down the other.

THE NORTHEAST

The dramatic beauty of northeastern Corfu begins above the bay of Ípsos and ends near Kassiópi, a lovely drive over a winding but well-paved road stretching some 20 km (12.5 miles). The road climbs sharply into the steep green slopes that guard the coast, offering tantalizing glimpses of the sea below. There are several viewing points along this cliffside road, but most of the shore is hidden and often accessible only by narrow, steep tracks that plunge alarmingly.

Some beaches can be reached only on foot. The best way to explore is by boat, which can be arranged from most jetties. It is worth noting that all the beaches from Ípsos to Kassiópi are of the pebble variety. Long-range, picture-perfect views often make these white-pebble beaches look like the white sands of the Caribbean, but this is not the case! Swimming is excellent at nearly all the beaches along this coast.

The transition from the commercialized resorts south of Ípsos Bay to the small, relatively less developed coves of the northeast peninsula comes at **Barbáti**. There is no steep track to negotiate here, just a gentle slope leading you down to sea level, where olive groves shelter a long, pebbly, and popular beach with all the usual watersports. The mountains rise steeply behind the beach, making an attractive backdrop. There is some music from beachside and roadside bars, but the atmosphere of Barbáti is very different from that of its southern neighbors.

By contrast in terms of size, the next resort along the cliffside road is **Nissáki**, where you must veer down steeply off the main road. The water here is a crystal-clear medley of greens and blues, though there is hardly room to spread your towel on its tiny pebble beach. It is undoubtedly a lovely spot, with two attractive tavernas and a shop selling arts, crafts, and souvenirs, but you will have to get here early (or late) to stake a beach claim.

Just a bit farther on, **Kamináki** is a strong contender for the title of "Corfu's most terrifying beach descent." There are two tavernas, a small watersports facility, and around 100 m (333 ft) of attractive white-pebble beach. The next beach along the road is home to the large Sol Nissáki Beach Hotel. You will have to share the pebbles with hotel guests. But the beach is of reasonable size, and because of the hotel there are good watersports facilities.

Drive a little farther, and at a tight hairpin turn there are signs pointing down to **Agni**. Because parking space below is so limited, it is best to ignore this road and arrive at Agni by boat from Nissáki or Kalámi. Agni is a glorious spot, known to lots of happy diners, many of who come here year after year to the three excellent tavernas that sit right on the picturesque beach. There are very few accommodations

---

A Glimpse of Albania

All along its northeast coast, Corfu looks across at the mainland of Albania. At its nearest point — on the stretch between Kalámi and Ágios Stéfanos — the shore of this mysterious ex-communist land is less than 3 km (1.8 miles) away. Its desolate, denuded slopes are a most impressive sight, particularly in the early evening, when the setting sun turns them into glorious shades of purple.

Before the recent troubles in the Balkans, tourist excursions from Corfu regularly set sail for Albania. But Albania is now deemed too dangerous for tourists to visit, and all excursions have stopped. However, a business service continues from Corfu Town.

here, and because of its relatively difficult access it is usually quiet even in high summer.

Lawrence Durrell's beloved White House still stands at the peaceful far side of **Kalámi**. It is now part holiday home, part taverna, where you can enjoy the marvelous landscape that inspired him to write *Prospero's Cell* (a largely evocative holiday read that describes Corfu in the days before tourism) in 1939. Despite a number of vacation villas and an insensitive new hotel complex that defaces one side of the glorious steep and verdant hills enclosing the bay, it remains at heart a tranquil resort. Various watersports are available.

On the neighboring bay, charming **Kouloúra** is scarcely large enough for a handful of fishing boats and a small taverna, but it is one of the most picturesque and photographed corners of Corfu. A constant stream of buses, cars, and motorbikes pull up at the large parking space high above on the main road to gaze down on its classic, tiny horseshoe harbor enclosed by tall cypresses. There is not a more typically Ionian view in the archipelago. Gerald Durrell, the brother of Lawrence, lived in Kouloúra and, while there, penned the amusing *My Family and Other Animals*.

Just past Kouloúra, yet another lovely white-pebble beach resort, far below, beckons invitingly to drivers from the cliffside road. It belongs to **Kerásia**, an attractive low-key resort with a handful of villas. It is reached by the turnoff to Ágios Stéfanos.

Sometimes dubbed "Kensington-on-Sea" after the well-heeled British visitors who holiday here, **Ágios Stéfanos** is the most exclusive of this coast's beautiful bays. Fishing boats and yachts bob lazily in the circular harbor, ringed by whitewashed cottages and tavernas. Although with each new year this charming resort becomes less of a secret, the laid-back atmosphere of a timeless fishing village still prevails.

Not so long ago, **Kassiópi** was also a quiet fishing village. These days it's a highly popular mass-market resort. In fact, Kassiópi was a thriving settlement even in Roman times, visited by Cicero, Cato, and Emperor Nero, among others. It is named for the god Kássios Zeus, protector of the remote corners of a land, and the village church supposedly stands on the site of a temple built in his honor. Its successor, the delightful Church of Panagía Kassiopítissa (Our Lady of Kassiópi), used to be the foremost shrine on Corfu before the arrival of St. Spyrídon. Its icons attest to the many miracles worked here. Opposite the church — on the site of an earli-

er castle — the Angevins built a now-ruined medieval fortress in the 13th century to provide protection against barbarian raiders.

While today the town is increasingly packed with tourists during the summer peak, the horseshoe-shaped harbor is still home to local fishermen, who carry on business as usual. Nightlife is lively, and Kassiópi has something of a party image with its tacky tourist bars. However, there are still

This church still stands in Períthia, though most residents have moved on.

several good authentic Greek restaurants, some nice craft shops, and an irresistible bakery. Four pebbly beaches give access for bathing and watersports in Kassiópi's small, rocky bays.

The spectacular coast road ends just before Kassiópi, and beyond it the scenery alters. Softer, shrub-covered foothills border a broad coastal plain blessed with an abundance of hayfields, vines, and almond trees. Here the first sandy beach, **Kalamáki**, appears, eagerly seized upon by tour operators who run excursions to "Sandy Beach," as they have renamed it. In reality it is an unattractive place, as dull as its gray sand.

Give it a miss and continue on to **Ágios Spyrídon**, 3 km (1.8 miles) farther north. This pretty, small beach with fine golden sand is something of a secret, with just one taverna and a handful of villas. It is backed by the Andinioti Lagoon, which is used as a fish farm.

An interesting break from the seaside is provided by the "ghost town" of **Old Períthia**, set on the northern slopes of Mount Pantokrátor and accessible at a turning opposite the road to Ágios Spyrídon. (Maps showing the road as unpaved are out of date.) Incredibly, Old Períthia was once the capital of Kassiópi province. Today there is just one family left, operating a charming tavern with a beautiful view of the crumbling village and, above it, Mount Pantokrátor. Simply sitting and savoring the peace and quiet here makes a journey well worthwhile.

No natural disaster overtook Old Períthia: Its residents simply moved to the coast in search of work. Overgrown footpaths between the crumbling stone houses and churches provide a haunting glimpse of old Corfiote life. In spring this valley is a great spot for naturalists, who can spot hundreds of butterflies, birds, and wildflowers. There is a path to the top of Mount Pantokrátor from Old Períthia; the climb takes about an hour.

THE NORTH

The shores of the north coast boast an 8-km (5-mile) expanse of sand stretching from Cape Róda through Acharávi and beyond to Cape Ágios Ektarini. It is not perfect by any stretch of the imagination, being narrow and of poor quality in many parts. The sea is very shallow for a long way out, making it popular with families but not too good for swimming.

From the main highway, a number of side roads go down to the relatively quiet, undeveloped Almyrós beach. A little farther on, marked by roadside sprawl, is **Acharávi**, a fast-growing resort of little character. The most noteworthy part is the "Old Village," set across the road from the beach and signposted by a waterpump on a traffic island in the middle of the road.

The neighboring resort of **Róda** is quite heavily developed but has considerably more character, with several older buildings and a pretty little square still surviving among the tavernas, gift shops, and touristy restaurants. The remains of a fifth-century B.C. Doric temple have been discovered here,

Canal of Love

The most famous of Sidári's many rock formations is the Canal d'Amour. Legend has it that anyone who swims through this narrow channel (when the water is in shade, according to some versions) will find the man or woman of their dreams. The problem is that the original Canal d'Amour, topped by a sea arch, collapsed long ago, and today nobody can quite decide which is the "official" Canal d'Amour. If you are in search of love, take no chances and swim through them all!

but despite a signpost there is nothing to see.

The booming resort of **Sidári**, 39 km (24 miles) from Corfu Town, is by far the most developed on the north coast, and its main street reflects many of the less savory aspects of mass tourism on the island. Nonetheless, even in the middle of such a relentless onslaught a picturesque little village square survives. Its charming church is worth a visit. The broad, sandy main beach has very shallow warm water with a wide range of watersports. Sidári's finest feature, however, is the series of striking **rock formations** that rise out of the sea at the western

Breath-taking Perouládes, the perfect vantage for enjoying a sunset.

end of the resort. The striated sandstone here is continuously carved by the wind and the sea into sandy coves with caves and ledges (some of which are very good for diving). There are a number of adjacent bays to explore, becoming more spectacular the farther west you go. At the last bay you can go no farther and, for your own safety, a fence blocks the top of the bluff. The view from here — of the giant cliffs tumbling straight down into the sea — is breathtaking.

From Sidári (and also from Ágios Stéfanos), boat trips run to the three small islands lying to the northwest, known collectively as the **Dhiapóndia Islands**. They are Mathráki, Eríkoussa, and Othoní and are famous for their fishing grounds. Othoní is the largest but is rarely visited; **Eríkoussa** has the best sandy beach and attracts the most visitors; Mathráki is the smallest, has a sandy beach, and is also an excursion destination. Each island has at least one taverna.

Stunning views of the northwestern tip of Corfu await at **Perouládes**, 2 km (1.2 miles) west of Sidári. Bear right at the end of the village, following the signs to the Sunset Taverna. At the end of the track, a flight of steps leading down to a remote beach reveals a glorious view of sheer, gold-gray striated cliffs plunging to the water, bordered by a delightful fringe of deep, dark sand. There are no facilities on the beach itself, but the Panorama Restaurant and Bar on the clifftop provides a fantastic place to watch the sunset. From the village, you can follow a footpath out to Cape Drástis, the island's northwestern tip, where you'll discover a pretty cove and a number of interesting offshore rock formations.

THE NORTHWEST

Ágios Stéfanos (not to be confused with the village of the same name on the east coast), also called San Stefano, is a developing resort with a long, wide beach of compacted sand and pebbles. It is popular with windsurfers and is still relatively uncrowded. Adjacent to the resort is a classic horseshoe-shaped fishing harbor where trips depart to the Dhiapóndia islands. A path leads out to the headland, which is the westernmost point in all Greece.

A 45-minute clifftop walk to the south leads to **Aríllas**, in the next bay (you can also drive there). This low-key resort is smaller and slightly prettier than many developments and has an attractive sandy beach that shelves gently into the sea.

A classic crescent-shaped beach of coarse sand stretches about 3 km (2 miles) around the bay at **Ágios Geórgios** and gives this burgeoning resort a lovely setting. Watersports are available, though the water is deeper and consequently much colder than at most other places on the island. Development is progressing apace, and this is the largest of the holiday centers in this corner of Corfu. But its relatively remote location and long beach mean that it never feels really crowded.

Paleokastrítsa

You can reach the most celebrated beauty spot on the island by a fast, paved road from Corfu Town; the distance is 25 km (15.5 miles). In the 1820s **Paleokastrítsa** was a favorite picnic spot for High Commissioner Sir Frederick Adam, and it is said that he had a road built across Corfu especially to reach it. (To justify the expense he proposed constructing a military convalescent home there, but it was never built!)

Many claim Paleokastrítsa was the site of the fabulous palace of King Alcinous, and its magnificent setting is indeed certainly fit for a king. Six small coves with incredibly clear turquoise water nestle in a coastline of hills and promontories draped in olive, cypress, and lemon trees. Strips of partly sandy, partly shingle beach ring the shoreline, and sea grottoes yawning out of sheer cliffs provide employment for the local boatmen who ferry visitors to and fro. Farther out to sea, a large ship-shaped rock known as Kolóvri is said to be the petrified Phaeacian ship that once bore Ulysses home.

Paleó, as it is often called, was never a village itself but merely the port of the hilltown of Lákones. The year-

round population is said to be less than 50, but this is hard to believe during the high season, when several hundred Corfiotes move down from their hillside homes to cater to the hordes of visitors who jam the hotels and villas.

Fortunately, no building has been permitted to crowd the bright little monastery that perches on the main, wooded promontory. You must dress appropriately to enter, and suitable wraps are provided at the gate for women. Constructed during the 13th century after the discovery here of an icon of the Virgin Mary, the monastery was rebuilt following a fire in the 17th century. Today it is a lovely, peaceful haven, and many thousands of rolls of film have been spent on its delightful patio, where a charming, creamy-yellow, typically Ionian belltower — decked with pink bougainvillea — is set off by a brilliant blue sky. Its three bells represent the Holy Trinity. Visit in the evening when there are few visitors and the soft light is at its best.

The monastery at Paleokastrítsa features a tiny museum and beautiful views.

A tiny museum harbors ancient icons, vestments, and various oddities, including an old olive press, huge wine barrels, a giant clam, and some enormous bones. "Part of the skeleton of a huge sea monster which was killed by the crew of a French ship in 1860 in the waters by the monastery," enthuses the caption on the latter item. The poor creature was in fact probably a whale.

As you enter the monastery church, you will be given a candle to light; a donation is expected. Do make sure you visit the monastery shop before leaving. It is a lovely place to browse or buy.

Paleó's main beach is the most crowded, but from here you can take boat excursions to Corfu's only sea caves and grottoes, with their mysterious pink rocks and blue "eyes" — extremely deep holes that, with the play of sunlight, turn an incredibly deep blue color. A longer trip can be made north from Paleokastrítsa to Ágios Geórgios Bay. The boat departs from the easternmost bay, Agía Trias (which is probably the most attractive of all Paleó's bays). It is a beautiful voyage, chugging past jagged cliffs that dwarf your tiny vessel. If you are lucky, you might see the dolphins that often cavort in these waters.

The finest view of Paleokastrítsa is from a lookout point high above the coastline. A narrow asphalt road twists up through several hairpin bends to the precariously perched village of Lákones. A little farther on, at a café called — with some understatement — Bella Vista, is a magnificent panorama that ranks among the finest in Europe.

From Paleokastrítsa ("Old Castle") you can see the massive walls of **Angelókastro**, the medieval fortress constructed by Michael Angelos Komnenos in the 13th century. In 1537 several thousand Corfiotes held out against Ottoman attack in this impregnable citadel. You can usually drive to the foot of the castle and climb to the summit, though if there is scaffolding present it might be closed while safety work is being completed. The views from here are marvelous and — in a nice piece of historical symmetry — extend eastward to Corfu Town's Old Fort. Look for the cave chapel of Agía Kyriakí, with hermit cells carved out of the rock as well as traces of frescoes.

Continue on to **Makrádes**, where the main road is lined with souvenir shops and tavernas catering to tour buses. The village itself (off a side road to the left) is a brightly white-washed cluster of houses with many picturesque corners. Just beyond Makrádes, follow the steep, secondary gravel road (rutted in parts) to **Pagí**. The first reward is the stunning vista of Ágios Geórgios Bay you get before you arrive. The second is the timeless mountain village itself, crowned by an Ionian belfry.

Alternatively, you can continue along the main road as far as scenic Troumbétas Pass. *Troumbétas* means "trumpet," and the pass is so called after the musically minded officer in charge of the road construction team that built this highway. Apparently he liked to stand on the pass above and blow his trumpet to call the men to lunch. From here you have various options: double back to Pági and Ágios Geórgios via Arkadádes, head north to Sidári or Róda, or return to Corfu Town via Skriperó.

THE WEST

The wide Rópa Valley separates Paleokastrítsa from the central and southern beaches of the west coast. This former marsh was drained by the Italians during their brief occupation in World War II. It is now the island's agricultural heartland. Farther south down the west coast lie Corfu's best beaches, with wide stretches of deep, golden sand.

The Rópa River flows down through the valley and out to the sea at **Ermónes**, making the latter site yet another contender for the *Odyssey* legend. The bay is picturesque, but its small beach of shingle and pebble is not particularly attractive and is surrounded by hotel and bungalow developments. The main hotel runs a funicular service right down to the beach.

By contrast, **Myrtiótissa** was described by Lawrence Durrell, some 60 years ago, as "perhaps the loveliest beach in the world." Perhaps, perhaps not — but at the very least few can deny it is the loveliest in Corfu and surely among the very best in all the Greek islands. Moreover, it is virtually unchanged since Durrell's day, unsullied by any kind of development or watersport. Sheer cliffs covered with trees and shrubs drop directly to the sand, creating a sense of wonderful isolation that has led Myrtiótissa to become unofficially recognized as the island's nudist beach. Don't worry if you don't want to shed all your inhibitions: There are many more people here who are costumed than those who let it all hang out. The sand is soft and golden, and at both ends of the long beach curl rocky promontories offering marvelous snorkeling in crystal-blue water.

The beach is signposted. Because it's about an hour by foot from the nearest bus stop on the Pélekas–Vátos road so your own transport is a big advantage. The beach is signposted, though. Even by car, however, you will get only part of the way along the rough dirt track through the olive groves. Continue on the bumpy track for a kilometer or so to the area marked "car park." From here it is a 10- to 15-minute walk to the beach. Some cars go all the way down, although this is not recommended, not least because there is nowhere to turn. You might be able to cope with the vertiginously steep path all the way on a motorbike or scooter, but this is for experienced riders only.

The easiest way to reach Myrtiótissa is by boat. Excursions from Paleokastrítsa, Ermónes, and **Glyfáda** have swelled the number of bathers here, and its solitude is not as it was.

Adjacent to Myrtiótissa as the seagull flies, but a little way round by road, is another of the island's acclaimed beaches, Glyfáda. Against a backdrop of crumbling cliffs with rock formations at either end, this large sandy beach is one of the finest and most popular on the island. Swimming is superb; the water is initially shallow, but deepens farther out. Beware, however, as there can be a strong undercurrent at the northern end (as on many beaches along the west coast). Unlike the situation at Myrtiótissa, development at Glyfáda is relatively heavy. You'll find a large hotel, several tavernas, and all watersports. The beach is frequented by daytrippers from Corfu Town and other resorts.

A steep hill leads up from Glyfáda to the attractive village of **Pélekas**. Today it is busy and commercialized, full of travel agencies, restaurants, discos, and rooms for rent. Nonetheless, it is still an attractive place and makes a good coffee stop — if you can find a parking place. Follow the signpost to "Sunset" (referring to the Sunset Restaurant) to get to the famous **Kaiser's Throne**, just

Folk costumes on display at the History and Folklore Museum of Central Corfu.

above Pélekas. Set atop a slender pinnacle, this is a panoramic viewpoint where the German emperor, Kaiser Wilhelm, built a small telescope point to watch the spectacular sunsets. From here, at certain times of the year, the sun appears to slide diagonally down the hillside and into the sea. The views are excellent, from Paleokastrítsa in the west to Corfu Town in the east.

Until quite recently, **Pélekas beach** — one of the finest unsung beaches on the island — was (like Myrtiótissa) difficult to access. Now a steep but well-paved road from Pélekas drops all the way down to the sea in a couple of minutes. Like Myrtiótissa and Glyfáda, the beach here is an idyllic, wide stretch of soft golden sand with a rocky portion providing good snorkeling in crystal waters.

> *A caique (pronounced ka-EE-key) is a typical small Greek boat.*

With only a couple of tavernas, it is still largely undeveloped, but the price of its new paved road can be seen at the far end of the beach in the shape of a huge new white hotel.

The charmingly unspoiled hilltown of **Sinarádes** lies 5 km (3 miles) south of Pélekas. Go past the central square, and opposite the Venetian-style church tower you'll see signs to the **History and Folklore Museum of Central Corfu**. Set in a traditional Corfiote house, it is an authentic reconstruction of a village home recreating the period 1850–1950 and features two floors of furniture, costumes, craftsman's tools, and numerous interesting bygones. The star exhibit is a *papirela,* a specimen of the reed boats (made in *Kon Tiki* fashion) used on Corfu from prehistoric times until 1950. Take time to wander round the pretty flower-decked village and enjoy its quiet atmosphere.

The scenic bay of **Ágios Górdis**, surrounded by verdant slopes covered with orchards, olive groves, and market gardens, is punctuated by a gigantic erect rock rising from the water at the southern end — an excellent spot for snorkeling, as are the rocks at the northern end. This once-quiet spot, with its long sand-and-shingle beach, has become very crowded in high season.

EXCURSIONS

Both the idyllic island of Paxos (Paxí) and the nearby Greek mainland are easily accessible for daytrips. Corfu travel agents can provide you with information on such excursions and on ferry schedules if you wish to stay longer.

 Paxos

One of the most delightful island experiences in the Mediterranean awaits you just ten nautical miles south of Corfu. **Paxos**, the smallest of the seven principal Ionian Islands, starts its seduction even before your boat docks, with dark green hills and astonishingly clear aquamarine waters.

> It's okay to go topless on most beaches, but cover up elsewhere. It might be offensive to some of the local population.

This tiny, verdant island — approximately 11 km (7 miles) long and 5 km (3 miles) wide — has some 300,000 olive trees and 1,500 permanent residents. It is famous for the quality of its olive oil; to this day Paxos earns more from olives than from tourism.

Traveling around this quiet, uncommercialized island is rather like stepping back in time. Did Corfu look this way 40 or 50 years ago, before mass tourism? What is also striking is how tidy the island is. There is virtually no litter or roadside subbish, and houses, villas, shops and restaurants are maintained and painted as if in preparation for a competition for best-kept Greek island.

The clear, limpid waters off Paxos are irresistible. The island has no natural sandy beaches, though off the shingle strip at Lákka the bottom is pure sand. However, you'll find excellent swimming from flat rocks and numerous pebbly coves around the shoreline, even if many are secluded and accessible only by boat. There is a small strip of imported sand on the islet of Moggoníssi in the far south, but it is nearly always crowded.

The sea caves in the towering cliffs along the west coast are truly spectacular, and the blue water there is so totally dazzling in its intensity that snorkeling is something you won't soon forget. The sea depth off these sheer rocks plunges from 25 m to 90 m (82 ft to 295 ft), with fish of varying sizes gliding along in schools at different levels. The largest of these caves, Ipapandí, was said to be Poseidon's home. A modern legend has it that a Greek submarine hid here during World War II, venturing out on occasion to conduct its valiant operations. Soaring out of the sea along this stunning coast is the massive hulk of **Orthólithos** — a huge finger of rock that has been hewn out of the cliff face by the elements.

Peaceful Paxos often appeals to those who want to get away from it all. But this can be difficult in mid-summer, especially in the first three weeks of August, when the tiny island becomes a magnet for Italian tourists. Then, prices swell accordingly and accommodations are heavily booked. The island has only one hotel; other accommodations are in fairly upmarket villas and apartments, though visitors who want to stay only a few nights can often find rooms to rent in

A Chip Off the Old Block

According to Greek mythology, the sea god Poseidon created Paxos by striking off the southern part of Corfu to make a retreat for himself and his mistress, Amphitriti. Circe, the enchantress who in Homer's *Odyssey* detained Ulysses on her island and turned his men into swine, came from Paxos.

Longós makes a delightful destination on an excursion to the small island of Paxos.

private houses. In high season, however, it's sensible to book accommodations in advance.

If you are a daytripper you only get to spend only a couple of hours here. Normally you have a choice of an island tour on the minibus or the speedboat tour of the caves. But to do the island justice, you should visit on a scheduled ferry and plan to spend at least two nights — enough time to see all the island's highlights and savor its relaxed atmosphere.

From Corfu Town, there is at least one scheduled boat to Paxos each day during the tourist season. The journey takes anywhere from 90 minutes to 3 hours. There are also one-day excursions to Paxos and neighboring Antipaxos, most of which also visit Párga on the mainland. In the high season there is a daily caique service between Gáios and Párga, taking approximately 90 minutes.

Most boats arrive at **Gáios**, the small quayside capital of the island. The pretty waterfront square is lined with tavernas, shops, and charming weathered houses, while the handsome yachts of the jet-set fill the harbor. During the high season, the narrow streets of Gáios buzz with daytrippers.

Any tour of this tiny island will also take in the villages of Lákka and Longós. Both are delightful. **Lákka** is a pretty port situated around a horseshoe-shaped bay on the northern island shore, ideal for watersports. It's the island's sailing capital and has several charming cafés and tavernas as well as an aquarium displaying all the local marine life. Two of the best beaches are also here. From Lákka there is a pleasant walk to a lighthouse on the cliffs and — a bit farther — to the hilltop monastery of Ipapandí, where a delightful bell-tower provides scenic views.

Longós (also known as Loggós) is a tiny, traditional fishing village huddled around a lovely harbor. Here, too, you'll find nice tavernas and cafés.

There is a regular bus service between the three main settlements, though it operates only during the day and early evening. Scooter and motorbike hire is available. There are a handful of taxis, but it can be difficult (if not impossible) to find one late at night.

Walking around the island itself is sheer delight. Timeless tracks along stone terraces and through mature olive groves end in idyllic hamlets. Along the roadsides you'll come across abandoned stone cottages and old olive presses, as well as lovingly tended grape arbors, cactus, and bougainvillea in profusion. The surrounding hillsides are dotted with round stone towers of ruined windmills missing their sails.

A popular walk leads from Magaziá, in the center of the island, up to the tidy hilltop cemetery at the Ágii Apóstoli

(Holy Apostles) church, where there is a striking view of the chalk-colored Erimítis cliffs. Between Magaziá and Fontána stands the island's largest olive tree — it takes five men with outstretched arms to embrace the huge twisted trunk. This giant stands in an incredible grove of 500-year-old trees, all still producing fruit faithfully every two years.

Antipaxos

Antipaxos (Antípaxi) is a completely unspoiled island 3 nautical miles to the south of Paxos. By sailboat the journey from Gáios takes 30–40 minutes. Cloaked in vineyards, lapped by transparent turquoise water, Antipaxos is occupied by only a handful of permanent residents but attracts plenty of visitors who converge on the island's two beaches. Vríka has an arc of fine white sand in a little cove, with tavernas at either end and a few beach umbrellas for hire. The nearby bay of Voutoúmi has brilliant white stones along its coastal strip but a soft sandy bottom underwater; apart from one taverna on the hillside, there are no facilities.

Swimming at both Vríka and Voutoúmi is superb, but don't expect to enjoy the idyllic setting in solitude. Excursion boats continually drop off bathers throughout the day (though they rarely come ashore), and numerous private boats also moor offshore. In high season, these sweet little beaches are often sadly overcrowded.

 ## Párga

Párga is an exquisite bay and village on mainland Greece's northwest coast, just 13 km (8 miles) east of Paxos. Its magnificent crescent bay is backed by verdant hillsides and dotted by little offshore islands. As you enter by sea, watch for the tiny island of Panagía, rather far out in the bay, crowned by a lonely church.

Like Corfu, this is by no means "untouched Greece." Párga has been very commercialized for many years, with a profusion of restaurants, bars, and tourist shops, none of which are terribly different from those in Corfu. Yet, even after the picturesque, quiet charms of Paxos (excursion boats often visit the two consecutively, so comparison is inevitable), Párga is still a delight. Its spectacular setting and views and quiet narrow whitewashed streets have an appeal all their own.

A Venetian castle built in 1624 looms above the promontory immediately to the left of the town. The climb up Párga's steep streets to the castle is actually shorter than it looks from below and well worth the effort for the stupendous views. Be sure to follow the path around the crest of the hill for a look at the high walled ruins and for additional views of the next bay, which is home to a long, splendid golden-sand beach.

If you have a day or two to spend in Párga, take the popular boat trip up the Acherón, thought to be the mythological river Styx — the gateway to the underworld. It concludes at the Necromantíon, the Oracle of the Dead. Here, in an underground chamber, the ancient Greeks sought contact with the souls of the departed, under the auspices of Hades, the Lord of the Underworld.

Snorkellers take advantage of the pristine waters around pretty Antipaxos.

WHAT TO DO

SHOPPING

Prices are rising in Greece, and as a result you shouldn't expect great bargains on Corfu. In souvenir and gift shops you might find that some good-natured bargaining is tolerated if you are buying more than one item or spending a reasonable amount — but don't push it. Local profit margins have to cover not only the tourist months but also the off-season, when shops are often closed. Corfu is not the Middle East or Asia, and some shops have even put up signs saying "Fixed Prices" or "No Bargaining."

If you are not a resident of the EU, you might be able to claim back the 18 percent VAT (sales tax) included in the price of most goods (if you spend over 40,000 drs.). Ask for details at shops with "Tax-Free for Tourists" stickers.

A lace shop in Corfu Twon displays its lovely wares in an elaborate storefront window display.

Where to Shop

By far the best range and quality of shopping on the island are to be found in Corfu Town. Businesses open in the morning and, because of the ubiquitous "siesta," close for a few hours in the afternoon. On Tuesday, Thursday, and Friday all shops reopen around 5pm and stay open until around 10pm. Many shops, however, are open only in the mornings on Monday, Wednesday, and Saturday and don't reopen for the evening. In Corfu Town the elegant old-world atmosphere of evening shopping (even if you are only window browsing) is not to be missed.

There are also a number of specialist workshop outlets on the road from Corfu Town to Paleokastrítsa. These are worth a visit, particularly the Wood's Nest (for olive wood) and the Seminole Leather Workshop.

Best Buys

Gifts from the olive tree. Corfu's most plentiful commodity — its olive trees — provides the basis for many fine souvenirs. Local artisans carve a variety of attractive bowls, platters, trays, statuettes, jewelry, toys, and all sorts of other ingenious olive-wood oddities. However, there's more than wood to the venerable trees. The

> Be patient in shops, banks, tavernas, or any other service situation where you must wait. The Greeks are not noted for their urgency in such matters!

island's olives and high-quality olive oil are appreciated worldwide, and a small bar of olive oil soap, often tastefully gift-wrapped, is an ideal, inexpensive present.

Pottery, glass, and ceramics. Corfu is home to many talented potters and craftspeople. You'll come across some lovely ceramics, including museum copies (the shop in the Old Fort specializes in the latter).

A motorcycle is one speedy way to get around the narrow streets of Lakka.

Gold and silver. Silversmiths still create bowls and trays using the old patterns of their Greek and Venetian ancestors, beating out the silver much as they would have done centuries ago. Many of the jewelry designs are based on traditional forms that reflect the development of Greek civilization, including such classic symbols as the lion, dolphin, ram, and bull. Voulgáreos Street, off the Listón, is the place to find silver in Corfu Town.

Leather. Leather is one of the few areas where you can still get real bargains. Goods such as handbags, sandals, wallets, and belts are often very good buys in Corfu Town. Pantón Street is home to many young and creative fashion designers.

Weaving and embroidery. There's a good selection of handwoven and embroidered items. Colorful woolen shoulder bags called *tagári,* handwoven floor mats in muted colors, tablecloths, napkins, aprons, skirts, and blouses of lace and cotton (in particular those woven in Corfiote villages) are always popular. The best buys in this category are probably cotton needlework shawls and bedspreads. The village of Kassiópi is home to a traditional industry of lace and crocheted goods, with Princess Margaret of the British royal family among the customers.

Reproduction icons. These are on sale all over Corfu Town and range greatly in price according to size and quality. Icons are also sold at the monasteries at Mount Pantokrátor and Paleokastrítsa (the latter is a particularly attractive place to shop).

Other specialties. Kumquat liqueur is a specialty made from small Japanese oranges grown on Corfu. There are medium and dry varieties of this sweet, orange-colored drink, though the clear-colored extract is considered the best quality. It is sold throughout Corfu, and the Mavromatis factory on the Paleokastrítsa road is a popular stop with tour groups. You can also sample kumquats in the form of crystallized fruits.

> A night out in Corfu Town traditionally begins with the *vólta*, the evening stroll or promenade. It's at its best along the Listón.

Another particularly sweet treat worth trying is nougat of almonds or sugared nuts. In addition, the richness of the island's flora ensures that its famous honey always possesses a distinctive character. In the fruit and vegetable markets look for bags of herb and spices.

Corfu has its own wine producers, and you can purchase a number of local vintages on the island. Other drinks available include *oúzo* (the national drink) and Greek brandy. The most famous brandy is Metaxa, which is rated from three to seven stars according to its quality. Most local alcoholic drinks are very reasonably priced.

Other typically Greek souvenir ideas include strands of worry beads *(kombolóïa);* tapes or CDs of Greek folksongs; elaborate skewers for *souvláki;* or a *bríkia*, a long-stemmed copper coffee pot used for making real Greek coffee, which also makes a nice ornament.

ENTERTAINMENT

Greek Music and Dance

The Corfiotes' love of good music and dance runs deep. Wherever you are staying, you will almost certainly come across a "Greek Night," which generally comprises a (more-or-less) traditional meal, Corfiote music (usually live), and dancing. It is of course the latter that everyone

Style and substance — decked out in their colorful finery, these young Corfiotes get down to some traditional moves.

comes to see. Traditional Corfiote and national Greek dances are taught at an early age, and the dancers — be they specially hired performers, restaurant staff, or simply locals who want to do their bit — can almost always be relied on for an energetic performance.

Whereas some Greek island dances are a little staid, the Corfiote interpretation can be particularly exciting. Corfiote males revel in athletic, virile, fast dances with high-kicking Cossack-like steps and not a little bravado. Dancing in a ring of fire to the accompaniment of plate-smashing is quite typical. Another dance involves picking up a glass of wine with the mouth (no hands allowed) from a press-up position. The wine is downed with a jerk of the neck; more macho types bite a chunk out of the empty glass before tossing it contemptuously aside!

> You'll hear Greek dancers frequently shouting "Ópa!" It means "Look out!" or "Watch it!"

Another crowd pleaser is the *zeibékikos*. The spectators, clapping in time to the music, cheer on the dancer, who bends back and seems to pick up a heavy table only with his teeth. (If you watch closely, he's actually taking the table's weight on his chest and stomach.) Not content with picking up a mere empty table, expert practitioners extend this feat to a table with a chair on top, and some go for broke by getting a young child to sit on the chair on top of the table! It has to be seen to be believed.

By the end of the night, it is a fair bet that the dancers will have cajoled everyone up onto the floor to join in a version of the *sirtáki*, Greece's best-known group dance; steps are simplified for visitors.

All these dances are usually accompanied by the famous eight-stringed mandolin, the *bouzoúki*, which for many foreigners has become synonymous with all Greek music. In

Calendar of Events

The following are the most important island-wide celebrations. Those surrounding Carnival and Easter are held on moveable dates in March and April. There are additional local festivities from May through August.

1 January St. Basil's Day *(Protochroniá)*. St. Basil is the equivalent of St. Nicholas (or Santa Claus) and gives presents to the children.

6 January Epiphany *(Ton Theofaníon)*. In seaside parishes the priest or bishop blesses the waters by throwing a crucifix into the sea; boys dive to retrieve it.

25 March Greek Independence Day procession in Corfu Town.

Carnival Parades and festivities during the last days of Carnival.

Orthodox Sunday Procession of the holy relics of St. Theodóra Augusta (see page 39).

"Clean Monday" First day of Orthodox Lent *(Katharí Deftéra)*. In good weather everyone goes out for a picnic.

Holy Saturday Procession of St. Spyrídon's coffin.

Easter Sunday Fireworks, candle lighting, and celebrations with music and dance.

21 May Ionian Union Day *(Énosis ton Eptaníson)* marks the anniversary of the seven islands joining Greece in 1864.

11 August Feast day in honor of St. Spyrídon in Corfu Town, including procession of St. Spyrídon's coffin.

15 August Assumption Day.

November St. Spyrídon Day *(Agíou Spyrídonos)*, when everyone in Corfu who is named Spíro after the saint receives gifts on his name day. On the first Sunday in November, the saint's coffin is stood upright so the faithful can kiss his feet.

fact, the instrument (which is of Turkish origin) is a comparatively recent import to the island, though the haunting melodies of Mános Hadjidákis and Míkis Theodorákis have made it an intrinsic part of Greek — and Corfiote — folklore.

Authentic performances of songs and dances are staged at village festivals throughout the season, where young and old alike participate, dressed in the traditional costumes of their ancestors. If there is not one in your locality during your holiday, make the trip into Corfu Town on

> The best way to enjoy the coastline is by boat. You can rent all types of motorboats, from a small outboard to a 10-m (33-ft) caique.

Tuesday evenings in summer. "Cultural Evenings" are held in the Town Hall Square, St. Spyrídon Square, and Spilia Square, featuring folkdancing, classical music, and traditional music with a choir (all start at 8pm). Music, dance, and folklore performances are also staged regularly in the New Fortress. The dancers are a lovely sight in all their finery, even if you don't experience the rough-and-ready excitement of taverna dancing.

Corfu is indeed a very musical island. Part of the British legacy means that Corfu Town alone boasts 3 orchestras, with at least a dozen more spread over the island, representing in all more than 750 musicians, as well as a municipal choir and a chamber music group. Marching bands are a regular fixture at festivals, and Sunday concerts often take place during the summer on the Esplanade. The New Fortress also hosts guitar recitals, jazz performances, and classical concerts.

Theater lovers should note that there are regular summer performances (often of ancient Greek plays), either in one of Corfu Town's two fortresses or at the Mon Repos outdoor theater.

See *The Corfiote* for details of all concerts, traditional festivals, and theater, or pick up the cultural events leaflet from the airport or the Corfu Town tourist office.

Other Nightlife

All the major resorts around the island have music bars, karaoke bars, clubs, and discos. Kávos is home to the island's youngest and wildest nightlife, followed by Benítses, Ípsos/Pyrgi, and Sidári. Corfu Town has a lively nightlife strip of its own, placed discretely just outside the center along the main road to the north of the port, and is worth the short taxi ride if you're staying anywhere between Gouviá and Pyrgi.

Parasailing above the beaches of Corfu offers thrilling views of the coast.

The island has one casino (Tel. 0661 36540), housed at the Corfu Holiday Palace (formerly the Hilton) in Kanóni. It is open from 8pm until 2am and offers roulette, blackjack, baccarat, and chemin de fer. You must be 18 to enter, and everyone has to show a passport. Men are required to wear a jacket and tie.

SPORTS AND RECREATION

Snorkeling and diving. The water is of excellent quality among the island's innumerable rocky inlets, and you will find small, fascinating sea grottoes and offshore rocks by Paleokastrítsa, Sidári, and Peroulades. Paleokastrítsa, in fact, is considered to be one of Europe's best locations. Don't be put off by eelgrass at certain east-coast points; some of the most colorful fish lurk in these shallows. Corfu's coastal waters are deep and clear, allowing divers some superb views. All scuba-diving schools have qualified instructors who will choose dive locations according to the amount of experience you have. Extended boat trips are available for advanced divers. For the more advanced trips, or to go by yourself and

Greek Easter

Corfu is famous for staging the most colorful Easter (Páscha) celebration in Greece. Here it is often called Lambrí ("brilliance"), and the spectacle attracts throngs of Athenians and other mainlanders. Every church has its Good Friday procession. The best starts after nightfall, departing from the cathedral with the bishop, dignitaries, and Corfu's famous town bands.

On Holy Saturday morning, the body of the patron saint, Spyridon, is paraded at length around town. The spectacular pomp honors his miraculous intervention in 1553, which saved Corfu from famine. Then, at 11am, police clear streets. Suddenly pottery, old plates, vases, and other breakables are hurled from the upper stories of houses. One theory behind this old and unique Corfu custom is that it is supposed to show anger at Judas' betrayal of Jesus.

At midnight, when the bishop intones "Christós anésti" ("Christ is risen"), every electric light goes on, fireworks soar overhead, church bells ring, and — most memorably — everyone lights a candle. Easter has arrived. On Easter Sunday wine flows like water and men perform traditional Greek and Corfiote dances.

rent equipment, you will need to show a diving certificate. Most major resorts have reputable diving schools.

Watersports. Corfu has numerous schools where you can learn to water ski. Avoid the northern shore, however, as the winds here can be too strong. Boards and sails for windsurfing are available for hire at nearly every beach on the island where the right conditions prevail, and instruction is offered at many places. Parasailing has become very popular and is available at several beaches, as is jet skiing. The major watersports centers are at Dassiá and Ípsos, though water skiing and windsurfing are available almost everywhere.

Golf. The highly acclaimed Corfu Golf Course (Tel. 0663 94220) is rated as one of the best courses in the Mediterranean. It is situated next to Ermónes, in the Rópa Valley. The 18-hole course is likened to a links course, with water

hazards and a design that provide a real challenge for seasoned golfers. You can arrange lessons with qualified pros (it's best to book ahead), and clubs and other essentials are available for hire. You'll also find a good shop and clubhouse with a bar and restaurant.

Non-golfers can enjoy a bit of horseback riding at the Rópa Valley Riding Stables (same phone number as

Take the plunge! Kids will love the wet and wacky thrill rides at Aqualand.

Fun in the sun! From kayakking to swimming to soaking up the rays, Corfu is the outdoor enthusiast's dream.

the golf course), offering one- to two-hour rides in this beautiful valley.

Cricket. Cricket was introduced by the English and is now an integral part of the Corfu Town summer scene. Matches take place regularly on the Esplanade on Saturday and Sunday afternoons, usually attracting a number of enthusiastic spectators. Corfu clubs frequently play against visiting teams from Britain and Malta, among others. The season's top tournament is the European Cricket Championship (ECC); it involves teams from seven countries and is contested in mid-September. There are two other pitches: at the Rópa Golf Club and at Gouviá Marina. If you are a keen cricketer, it may be possible to play with one of the Corfu teams (Tel. 0661 47753).

ACTIVITIES FOR CHILDREN

Corfu is a very popular holiday spot for families, and most resorts and newer hotels are designed with children in mind.

Many larger hotels have separate, shallow children's swimming pools and play areas, and most of the large class-A hotels have special games and activity programs which will keep the children happily occupied.

While most beaches are perfectly safe for children, those with sandy shores and very shallow water will be most appealing to families with very young children. These include Róda, Sidári, Acharávi, Aríllas, and Kávos, though the latter is also known for its gregarious nightlife.

Corfu Town is largely for adults, but kids might enjoy a ride around town in the colorful 19th-century horsedrawn carriages. The *Kalypsó Star* glass-bottomed boat leaves the Old Port every hour for a 50-minute trip around Vídos Island, where (caged) sea lions perform for the passengers. In Paleokastrítsa the short boat trip to the caves and grottoes is also a winner with kids.

The most popular children's day out (and a great day for all splashaholics) is at the Aqualand water park, with many thrill rides, the gentle "Lazy River," the bouncy castle, swimming pools, and special children's play area. Located at Ágios Ioánnis, in the center of the island some 12 km (7.5 miles) west of Corfu Town, the park is open daily from April through October. It's quite expensive, but children under 4 are admitted free and there are reduced rates after 3pm (web site: <www.corfu-net.graqualand/>). Special buses make the trip from all over the island.

If your children love nature and horses, take them pony trekking, a good outing for the whole family that is suitable for all ages. This can be booked from most tourist agencies.

Most children love the spectacle of "Greek Night" entertainment, with whirling dancers, rings of fire, smashing plates, tables picked up with teeth, and other denture-defying acts. Most Greek Nights start around 10pm.

EATING OUT

Take an idyllic waterside setting, add charcoal-grilled fish, meat on a spit, and a crisp Greek salad, and you have the basic components of a typical Corfu meal. Greek cooking is usually very simple, with just a few basic ingredients and herbs for flavoring. Olive oil, tomatoes, onion, garlic, cheese, and lemon are all recurring themes.

If you tire of local fare, you can usually find (not too far away) everything from gourmet cuisine to ethnic fare, from hamburgers to crêpes and pizza. Don't turn your nose up at the latter — because of the Italian influence here, the pizza can be very good.

There is in theory little difference between an *estiatório* (restaurant) and a taverna, though any place with the latter name is likely to be more of a basic, traditional establishment. It used to be common practice for customers to enter the kitchen of a taverna and inspect the array of pots and pans on the stove to pick out their meal, but this

> Don't feed the cats, which are a feature of Greek tavernas. It just encourages them to beg and make a nuisance of themselves.

quaint "nothing-to-hide" custom is now the exception. The modern convention is simply to order from a menu, which is almost always printed in English (and usually at least one other major European language) in addition to Greek. Service is generally slow — sometimes excruciatingly so.

Greek food is no longer the bargain that it used to be, but meals are generally still much less expensive than in most of Western Europe. Government price controls operate for all categories of restaurant except deluxe. So it is not so much where you eat as what you eat (fish, for example, is usually expensive) that will decide the amount of the bill.

A service charge is included, but diners normally leave between five and ten percent extra for the waiter.

Corfiotes, like most other Greeks, enjoy their food warm rather than piping hot. Casserole dishes such as *moussaká* might be cooked at lunchtime and either kept warm all day or just reheated at night. If you like your food hot or if you are concerned about the hygiene implications of re-heatng, you should order grilled dishes in the evening.

WHAT TO EAT

Fast Food

For snacks or even lunch, many vacationers follow local example and pop into a bakery for a freshly baked *fílo*-pastry pie filled with cheese, a *tiropitákia*; if it's filled with spinach, it's a *spanakópita*.

Another cheap option often available as take-out food is a *gyro,* better known to Western Europeans as a *doner kebab.*

> **To attract your waiter's attention, call out "Parakaló!" ("Please!").**

Pressed meat is sliced off a vertically rotating spit and stuffed into *pita* bread with some salad, a yogurt dressing, and a handful of french fries (chips). A similar option is *souvláki:* a kebab of grilled cubes of meat, grilled over charcoal, and served in the same fashion. Souvláki is also popular served as a starter, or as a main course, in restaurants and tavernas.

Appetizers

There are a great many ways to start your meal. For a little of everything, try a plate of mixed appetizers *(mezédes).*

Dolmádes are vine leaves that have been stuffed with minced meat and/or rice and then seasoned with grated onion and herbs. *Melitzánes tiganités* are slices of aubergine (eggplant) fried in batter; *kolokithákia tiganitá* are courgette (zucchini) fritters. Another popular starter is *saganáki* (fried cheese).

The Greeks have a great predilection for dips, and Corfu is no exception. The commonest are the following: *tzatzíki,* yogurt with crushed garlic and grated or finely sliced cucumbers; *taramosaláta,* a smooth, pink paste made from gray mullet roe, mashed potatoes or moistened bread, olive oil, and lemon juice; and *melitzanosaláta,* a purple-brown mush of grilled aubergine (eggplant), onions, olive oil, and garlic. Dips are served with either local white bread or *pita* bread.

A street vendor serves up a fresh batch of deliciously sweet loukoumádes.

Saláta choriatíki ("village salad") is the proper term for the ubiquitous "Greek salad," eaten either as a starter or with the main course. It comprises tomatoes, sliced peeled cucumber, mild onions, black olives, and green peppers, topped with a thick slice or two of white féta cheese, drizzled with olive oil and dusted with oregano.

Fish and Seafood

Fresh fish abounds, but the seas around Corfu have been almost exhausted and restaurant prices are likely to shock many visitors. These are often quoted by weight, so to avoid any unpleasant shocks at the end of your meal establish what the price is before ordering.

A seafood specialty here is the pleasantly piquant *bourdéto:* white fish in a sauce of tomato, red pepper, and olive oil. *Bianco* (sometimes called *bouillabaisse)* is a catch-all name for a stew of local fish, potatoes, white wine, lemon, garlic, black pepper, onions, and whatever else the chef fancies throwing in.

There are several varieties of fish that have no English translation, such as the tasty *melanoúri* or *sargós. Barboúni* (red mullet), a Mediterranean favorite, is a popular fish on Corfu. Most fish are served simply grilled. More familiar are *fagrí* (sea bream), *glóssa* (sole), *sinagrída* (red snapper), and *xifías* (swordfish). A typical (though not exclusively Corfiote) accompaniment to battered fish is *skordaliá*, a garlic purée.

Seafood starters include *kalamaria* (squid) fried in batter; *maridákia* (whitebait) is also generally deep fried. You'll find *garídes* (prawns) and *oktapódi* or *chtapódi* (octopus) served *saganáki*-style, simmered in a piquant tomato sauce and topped with cheese.

Meat Dishes

Moussaká is perhaps the most popular of all Greek

It would be easy to eat a different seafood feast every night of your stay.

dishes (pronounced "moo-sah-**kah**" rather than "moo-**sah**-kah"). It is a layered dish of minced meat (traditionally lamb), aubergine (eggplant), potatoes, a béchamel-type sauce, and spices.

The Greeks love lamb. *Kleftiko* is traditional Greek oven-roasted lamb, though in Corfu the dish might be served in a sauce of wine, vegetables, and yogurt. Another popular lamb dish is *arní frikassé,* stewed with green vegetables. Less common is *gastra:* lamb baked in white wine sauce with garlic and red peppers.

Sofríto is an island special comprising slices of beef or veal stewed in a sauce of white wine, garlic, and wine vinegar with a touch of black pepper. *Stifádo* is beef stewed with baby onions in a finely spiced tomato sauce — something of an island specialty, though it is available all over Greece.

> If the waiter says "Kalí órexi!" he is wishing you "Bon appetit!"

Stamna is another beef casserole, baked with courgettes (zucchini), peppers, and cheese in a ceramic dish.

More adventurous diners might like to try *kokorétsi:* spiced sausages of innards flavored with herbs. *Keftédes* are Greek meatballs, usually made from minced beef or lamb, flavored with grated onion, spices, and herbs.

One of the cheapest menu items is *kotópoulo* (chicken), often simply roasted on a spit over charcoal. Pork usually comes simply as pork chops, but *afelia* — a tender pork stew made with red wine, cumin, and coriander seeds — is well worth a try. In addition, you'll nearly always find steaks and chops.

Pasta Dishes

The Greeks and especially the Corfiotes are very fond of pasta. *Pastítsio* is an island specialty with layers of minced meat,

Nature's bounty — a selection of just some of the fruits you'll find during your stay on Corfu.

tomato, macaroni, and béchamel sauce topped with cheese. *Youvétsi* is a similar meat and pasta combination (usually with lamb), baked in a clay casserole. Don't confuse *pastítsio* with *pastitsáda;* the latter is beef stewed in a richly flavored tomato sauce, served with pasta.

Vegetables

Vegetarians will not have the best of times in Corfu. Chips (french fries) and Greek salad are the principal accompaniments to meals. However, you'll usually find *hórta* (spinach-like wild greens); *fasólia* (butter beans), often described as *gigantes* ("giant beans") and served in a delicious tomato-and-onion sauce; and *fasolákia* (string beans). Not to be missed is *briam,* often described as "Greek ratatouille," consisting of peppers, courgettes, tomatoes, onions, and olive oil; it's served as appetizer, side dish, or main course (perhaps topped with cheese and breadcrumbs).

Desserts

Sweets are just that — and usually sticky as well. The most famous is *baklavá,* a flaky, paper-thin *fílo* pastry filled with chopped almonds and walnuts and drenched in honey or syrup. Similar is *kataïfi,* a pastry that resembles shredded wheat. You will not see these in a restaurant or taverna. Look instead in bakeries or in a *zaharoplasteío,* a café/patisserie (usually found only in Corfu Town). Yet another mouth-watering specialty is *loukoumádes,* a kind of sweet, puffy deep-fried donut dipped in syrup. It is often sold by street vendors.

A much healthier food is Corfu honey *(méli),* which makes a wonderful breakfast snack poured onto the island's local yogurt *(giaoúrti).* You'll find this on restaurant menus, usually with nuts added for a bit of crunch and extra flavor. It's also delicious with fruit, especially peaches.

Corfu's magnificent wild strawberries *(fráoules),* which appear in May and June, are another of the tastiest treats in the Ionian. For much of the summer, however, the only fruits that appear on the restaurant table are yellow melons, watermelons, and grapes.

Ginger Beer

Corfu Town is the only place in Greece where you can get genuine 19th-century-style ginger beer, a delightful relic of British colonial rule. Locally called *tzinzerbíra* (pronounced "tsin-tsi-BEE-ra"), it should be served well chilled and is extremely refreshing in the hot weather.

WHAT TO DRINK

Coffee

If you order simply "coffee," you might well be offered the traditional Greek brew, *kafés ellinikó* — a thick, strong concoction brewed to order in a long-handled copper or aluminum pot called a *bríkia* and poured (grounds and all) into a tiny cup. It is typically served very sweet *(gliko)*, with sugar already added. If you want just a little sugar, ask for it "medium" *(éna métrio)* or "without sugar" *(éna skéto)*. A glass of cold water is usually served with the coffee.

If you prefer instant coffee, ask for *nes* or *neskafé* — or ask for "milk coffee" *(kafé me gála)*. These days more places are also serving filter coffee and/or Italian-style cappuccino and espresso.

A real treat in hot weather, and quite a fashionable drink too, is *frappé* — Greek iced instant coffee. The milky version looks a little like a small Guinness and tastes like a coffee milk shake, but it's surprisingly refreshing. Most Corfiotes drink their frappé black.

Izinzerbíra, Corfu's delcious ginger beer, always hits the spot on a hot day.

Alcoholic Drinks

Oúzo, the national aniseed-flavored aperitif made from dis-tilled grape detritus, is very often taken neat *(skéto)* on Corfu. When you add the cold water that always accompanies it, the oúzo turns milky — and becomes rather less potent.

Corfu produces a reasonable quantity of local wine, but most of this is kept by the vineyard owners for their own private use. Usually light red *(kokkinéli)* or deep purple in color, it is best drunk cool from the cellar, where it sits in wooden casks.

House wine is usually of poor quality. It is nearly always worth paying a few drachmas more for a better wine from the mainland. Among local bottled wines, the rarest and most expensive is Theotóki, a dry white wine produced solely from grapes cultivated in the Rópa Valley. More common is the wide range of mainland Greek wines to choose from. Three top-class reds are Cáva Tsántali, Cáva Boutári, and Calligás Montenéro. Those who prefer white or rosé might try Tsántali's Agiorítiko and Macedónian brands or Boutári Lac des Roches, which is a smooth white. At the end of a meal, Mavrodáphne — a sweet red similar to Marsala — is a good choice.

> "Real" Greek men drink their *oúzo* straight. As a visitor, you should water it down a little — at least to start with!

Retsína is, to put it mildly, an acquired taste, and it's less popular on Corfu than elsewhere in Greece. But you'll have no trouble finding this inexpensive pine-resin white wine.

The Ionian Islands are well known for their liqueurs. The specialty of Corfu is *koum kouat* (kumquat), a syrupy con-fection that is produced from miniature kumquat oranges, grown here far from their native Japan.

The common drinking toasts are "Yámass!" or "Yássas!" ("To health!").

To Help You Order...

Could we have a table?		**Tha boroúsame na échoume éna trapézi?**	
I'd like a/an/some…		**Tha íthela…**	
beer	**mía bíra**	napkin	**petseta**
mineral	**metallikó**	potatoes	**patátes**
water	**neró**	rice	**rízi**
(iced)	**(pagoméno)**	bread	**psomí**
water	**neró**	coffee	**éna kafé**
cutlery	**macheropírouna**	dessert	**éna glikó**
salad	**mía saláta**	fish	**psári**
soup	**mía soúpa**	fruit	**froúta**
sugar	**záchari**	glass	**éna potíri**
tea	**éna tsäi**	ice cream	**éna pagotó**
milk	**gála**	meat	**kréas**
wine	**krasí**		

...and Read the Menu

barboúnia	red mullet
briám	"Greek ratatouille"
chtapódi	octopus
fasólia	beans
garídes	prawns
keftédes	meatballs
kléftiko	roast lamb
kotopoulo	chicken
dolmádes	stuffed vine leaves
marídes	whitebait
pastítsio	macaroni pie
sofríto	veal stew
souvláki	kebab
stifádo	stew (usually beef) with tomatoes

HANDY TRAVEL TIPS

An A–Z Summary of Practical Information

A

ACCOMMODATIONS

Many hotels are heavily booked with package tours from mid-June until October, especially during the first three weeks of August. Reservations are strongly recommended. If you do arrive without one, go to the information center in Corfu Town (see tourist information). Although not an accommodations booking agency, it does have a list of all Corfu hotels and might be able to point you in the right direction. You might also check the Internet at <www.greekhotel.com>.

Prices are controlled according to a rating system compiled by the National Tourist Organization of Greece (E.O.T), based on a building's age, facilities, amenities, and other factors. Hotels are rated from A to E (rooms in categories A–C have private bathrooms), but prices can vary widely within each category. Luxury establishments, rated L, are not price-controlled.

In high summer season some form of air-conditioning is vital for a good night's sleep. If your room doesn't have air-conditioning (and many older properties don't), you can rent fans locally.

Villas and apartments. Corfu has more villas, apartments, and studios (the latter terms are interchangeable) for rent than do many other Greek tourist centers. Accommodations range from simple rooms to lavishly appointed summer homes — often tastefully converted from a traditional house or houses — complete with swimming pool. In the UK, four companies specialize in top-of-the-range secluded luxury villas on both Corfu and Paxos: CV Travel (Tel. 0870 606 0013), Simply Ionian (Tel. 0208 995 1121), Greek Islands Club (Tel. 01932 220 477), and Corfu à la Carte (Tel. 01635 201 140). More affordable are Meon Villas (with a good selection across the island; Tel. 01730 268 411), Direct Greece (with nice properties on the northeast coast at very reasonable prices and excellent representatives on the ground; Tel. 0208 785 4000), Something Special (also specializing in the northeast, with pools at all villas; Tel. 01992 557 755). Note that callers from outside the UK should not dial the initial 0 in these British numbers.

Rooms in private homes. The cheapest rooms are those that are privately rented. They are almost always clean, but you'll rarely have your own shower and toilet. They are graded A to C by the local tourist police, though rates are often somewhat negotiable.

I'd like a single/double room.	**Tha íthela éna monó/dipló domátio.**
with bath/shower	**me bánio/dous**
What's the rate per night?	**Piá íne i timí giá mía níkta?**

AIRPORT (ΑΕΡΟΔΡΟΜΙΟ — *aerodrómio*)

Located only 1 km (0.6 mile) from the capital, Corfu's lagoon-side airport is capable of handling all but the largest jets. However, time spent here is rarely anything less than frustrating, with long waits for baggage and other inconveniences.

Here are some tips for surviving the airport departure pandemonium. Take your own drinks and sandwiches, as delays are commonplace and the refreshment outlets cannot cope. Facilities and seating in the airside lounge are inadequate, so the best place to find a space to sit down is at the far end of the hall in "Arrivals."

The terminal building has shops, car-rental desks, and refreshment places (the latter are liable to close just as you get to the head of the line). The currency-exchange office opens at 9am and remains in operation until 2am if there are international flights scheduled to land late at night. (It's a good idea to buy Greek currency before traveling, in case the airport office is closed.)

There is no bus service linking the airport with Corfu Town. Taxis in theory are inexpensive (about 2,000 drs. to Corfu Town), but be forewarned that overcharging on the airport route is common.

For general airport information: Tel. 0661 30180. For international flight information: Tel. 0661 38694. For domestic flights: Tel. 0661 38695.

B

BICYCLE and MOTORCYCLE RENTAL/HIRE (ΕΝΟΙΚΙΑΣΕΙΣ ΠΟΔΗΛΑΤΩΝ/ΜΟΤΟΠΟΛΗΛΤΩΝ — *enikiásis podiláton/motopodiláton*)

You can rent bicycles and motorcycles in all the tourist centers. Many package operators, however, warn clients against motorized cycles and scooters for the quite legitimate fear of an accident. It is vital that you check that motorcycle rental does not invalidate your holiday insurance. Moped and scooter rental is cheap (starting at around 5,000 drs. per day, including third-party insurance (CDW: collision damage waiver).

Terms vary by operator. Usually, to rent a motorcycle with an engine larger than 75 cc you must be at least 18 years of age and hold a full driver's license. Note that it is illegal to ride without a crash helmet. In practice very few people wear them, but the law is being enforced and spot fines are often issued.

It is certainly not advisable to ride a motorcycle in shorts or a swimsuit (as so many people do), since burns or scrapes resulting from even a slight accident could be appalling. Inspect brakes and tires before renting, and drive with care. Even on good roads there is the occasional pothole.

Bicycle rental is less common, largely because of Corfu's mountainous terrain, but a good place for serious bikers is the Corfu Mountain Bike Shop (Tel. 0661 93344 or 0661 97609), on the main road at Dassiá. They offer top quality bikes and can organize expeditions.

What's the rental charge for a full day? **Póso kostizi giá mía iméra?**

BUDGETING for YOUR TRIP

Corfu is certainly not the cheapest of the Greek Islands. It is probably as expensive as (if not a bit more expensive than) most other Mediterranean destinations. In the high season, the rate for a good four star hotel is around 25,000–30,000 drs. per night for a double room. As always, booking an airfare/accommodations package (particularly at the last minute) will make a substantial saving.

Dining is not as cheap as you might think, with a three-course meal plus drinks in a decent restaurant or taverna coming to around 6,000 drs. per person. Car hire starts from around 10,000 drs. per day in high season (including fully comprehensive insurance). Public transport and museum fees are inexpensive.

C

CAMPING (KAMΠIΓΚ — *camping*)

Camping in Greece is permitted at official sites only. There are 12 sites listed by the E.O.T., all open at least from April to October. For the list, contact the tourist office in Corfu.

May we camp here? **Boroúme na kataskinósoume edó?**

We have a tent. **échoume míaskiní**

Corfu

CAR RENTAL/HIRE (ΕΝΟΙΚΙΑΣΕΙΣ ΑΥΤΟΚΙΝΗΤΩΝ — *enikiásis aftokiníton*)

It is definitely worth renting a car in order to explore the wonderful island scenery. As throughout Greece, this is not particularly cheap, but it is certainly cheaper than touring by taxi. And public transport is inadequate for island sightseeing. For a decent family-sized car in high season, you should budget around 100,000 drs. per week. In high summer choose a model with air-conditioning.

You'll find car-rental firms at the airport and throughout the island, especially in tourist centers. To be on the safe side, reserve a car ahead of time — especially for the high season. Local firms generally charge slightly less than international agencies and provide equally good cars and service. International firms include Avis, Hertz, and Budget.

You will need a credit card for the deposit and a full national license (held for at least one year) from your country of residence. Depending on the model and the rental company, the minimum age for renting a car varies from 21 to 25. Third-party liability insurance (CDW) is usually included in the stated rate, and it is always worth paying a little more for comprehensive coverage.

I'd like to rent a car (tomorrow) **Tha íthela na nikiáso éna aftokínito (ávrio).**

CLIMATE

The months of July and August are the sunniest and warmest on Corfu — and attract the most tourists. You may prefer to stay between mid-May and late June or from early September to mid-October. Be aware that at any time outside July — even in August — you might see rain. Corfu is, after all, one of the greenest of all the Greek islands. In winter it rains very hard.

December is Corfu's rainiest month and January its coldest month, but even during these mid-winter doldrums the climate is temperate. Spring, when Corfu bursts with wildflowers, is the best time for walking.

	J	F	M	A	M	J	J	A	S	O	N	D
air temp. C	10	10	12	15	19	24	27	26	23	19	15	12
air temp. F	50	50	54	59	66	75	81	79	73	66	59	54
sea temp. C	15	15	15	16	18	21	24	25	24	21	19	18
sea temp. F	59	59	59	61	64	70	75	77	75	70	66	64
daily hours of sunshine	5	6	7	7	9	10	11	12	9	6	4	3

CLOTHING

Clothing is almost always casual on Corfu. Unless you plan to frequent the casino, you can leave ties and fancy dresses at home. However, it is quite nice to dress up a little for a night in Corfu Town and, after dark, you might appreciate a wrap, a light jacket, or a sweater (with the exception of midsummer).

Choose lightweight cotton clothing in spring and summer, and a warm jacket, sweater, and rainwear in autumn and winter. Since it does rain from time to time on Corfu, some sort of protective coat or an umbrella is a good idea — except for July. Plastic sandals are useful for stony beaches.

CRIME and SAFETY

(see also EMERGENCIES and POLICE)

The Corfiotes, like the vast majority of Greek people, are scrupulously honest. Unfortunately, however, thefts occur more often than they used to on the island, so it's sensible to leave valuables in the hotel safe. Take care of your passport.

Corfu

Possession of drugs is a serious matter in Greece. Make sure you have a prescription from your doctor if you will be carrying syringes, insulin, any narcotic drugs, or even codeine, which is illegal in Greece.

Any fears about the proximity of Corfu to Albania and unrest in the Balkans are, for the vast majority of vacationers, groundless.

CUSTOMS and ENTRY REQUIREMENTS

Visitors from EU countries need only an identity card to enter Greece. Citizens of most other countries must have a valid passport. European and North American residents are not subject to any health requirements. In case of doubt, check with a Greek consulate or embassy in your own country before departure.

You should be aware that certain prescription drugs (including some tranquilizers and headache preparations) may not be carried into the country without a prescription or official medical document.

Currency restrictions. Nonresidents may import up to 100,000 drs. and export up to 40,000 drs. (in denominations no larger than 5,000 drs.). There is no limit on the amount of foreign currency or traveler's checks you may import or export as a tourist, though amounts in excess of $1,000 or its equivalent should be declared to the customs official upon arrival if you wish to take them out without problems when you leave.

I have nothing to declare.	**Den écho na dilóso típota.**
It's for my personal use.	**Íne giá prosopikí chrísi.**

DRIVING

Road conditions. Main roads are generally very good, though curves in the road are sometimes indicated too late — or not signposted at all — and they are never banked. If there is a mirror on a bend, slow down to first gear — it is probably going to be extremely tight or narrow, or both! Use great care at all times.

On many clifftop roads it is very dangerous to pass Be patient if there is a slow-moving bus or heavy vehicle in front of you (it seems there always is!). Conversely, try to let local speed maniacs pass you as soon as it is safe to do so.

Secondary roads are usually fine, though anything marked "unsurfaced" on a map can be very rough. Rockslides are common in the rainy season, and broken shoulders or potholes are not unknown on even the best-paved stretches. Drive with extreme caution, as you might be responsible for damage sustained to the underside of your rental car, even with comprehensive coverage.

Driving regulations. Drive on the right side and pass on the left. Traffic from the right has right of way. If a driver flashes the lights, it normally means "Stay where you are," not "Go ahead." Seat belts are obligatory. The speed limit is 80 km/h (50 mph) inside built-up areas, 100 km/h (62 mph) outside. In practice, however, Corfu's winding roads usually set the speed limit.

Fuel. Unless you are on the top of Mount Pantokrator, you will never be far from a filling station. In rural areas, however, they are open in the morning only and closed on Sundays. On busy main roads and in resorts, they open daily from early until late.

If you need help. For breakdown and accident assistance, phone the Greek motoring club (E.L.P.A.) at 0661 39504. In case of road emergency, dial 104.

Road signs. Road signs on main roads and at junctions are in both Greek and Latin (Western) letters, but on secondary roads they might be in Greek only:

Corfu

ΑΔΙΕΞΟΔΟΣ	No through road
ΑΛΤ/ΣΤΟΜ	Stop
ΑΝΩΜΑΛΙΑ ΟΔΟΣΤΡΩΜΑΤΟΣ	Bad road surface
ΑΠΑΓΟΡΕΥΕΤΑΙ Η ΕΙΣΟΔΟΣ	No entry
ΑΠΑΓΟΡΕΥΕΤΑΙ Η ΣΤΑΘΜΕΥΣΙΣ	No parking
ΔΙΑΒΑΣΙΣΠΕΖΩΝ	Pedestrian crossing
ΕΛΤΤΩΣΑΤΕ ΤΑΧΥΤΗΤΑ	Reduce speed
ΕΠΙΚΙΝΔΥΝΗ ΝΟΣ ΚΑΤΩΦΕΡΕΙΑ	Dangerous incline
ΕΡΓΑ ΕΠΙ ΤΗΣ ΟΔΟΥ	Roadworks in progress
ΚΙΝΔΥΝΟΣ	Caution
ΜΟΝΟΔΡΟΜΟΣ	One-way traffic
ΠΑΡΑΚΑΜΠΤΗΡΙΟΣ	Diversion (detour)
ΠΟΡΕΙΑ ΥΠΟΧΡΕΩΤΙ ΚΗ ΔΕΞΙΑ	Keep right

Are we on the right road for… ?	**ímaste stosostó drómo giá… ?**
Full tank, please.	**Na to gemísete me venzíni.**
normal/super/unleaded	**aplí/soúper/amólivdos**
My car has broken down.	**Épatha mía vlávi.**
There's been an accident.	**Égine éna disteíchima.**

Fluid measures

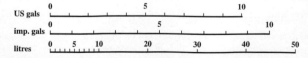

Distance

km	0	1	2	3	4	5	6		8		10		12		14		16
miles	0	½	1	1½	2		3		4		5		6	7		8	9	10

E

ELECTRICITY

Corfu has 220-volt/50-cycle AC current. Sockets are two-pin continental style. Adapters are not that common, so it is best to bring one with you.

an adapter   **éna metaschimatistí**

EMBASSIES and CONSULATES *(presvía; proxenío)*

There are British and Irish consular offices in Corfu Town. Embassies of all major countries are located in Athens. From outside Greece, first dial the country code 30 before the appropriate number.

British Consulate: corner of Alexándras Avenue and Meneurátes Street (on seafront), Corfu Town, Tel. 0661 30055.

Irish Consulate, 20a Kapodistríou Street,Corfu Town; Tel. 0661 32469.

Embassies:

Australia: D. Soútsou 37, 115-21 Athens; Tel. (01) 645 0404.

Canada: Gennadíou 4/Ipsilántou, 115-21 Athens; (01) 727 3400.

Ireland: Leofóros Vas. Konstantínou 7, 106-74 Athens; Tel. (01) 723 2771.

New Zealand: Xenia 24, 115-28 Athens; Tel. (01) 771 0112.

Corfu

South Africa: Leofóros Kifissías 60, 151-25 Maroússi; Tel. (01) 680 6645.

UK: Ploutárchou 1/Ipsilántou, 106-75 Athens; Tel. (01) 723 6211.

US: Leofóros Vas. Sofías 91, 115-21 Athens; Tel. (01) 721 2951.

EMERGENCIES

Police (Corfu Town), all-purpose emergency number: **100**.

Corfu Town hospital: 0661 45811/5 (5 lines).

Ambulance service: **166** or 0661 39043.

Fire: **199**.

Vehicle emergency: **104**.

Fire!	**Fotiá!**
Help!	**Voíthia!**
Police!	**Astinomía!**
Stop!	**Stamatíste!**

G

GETTING THERE

It is possible to cross Europe overland and take the ferry from Italy to Corfu. But for the vast majority of visitors, air travel is the only practical route. Most take charter flights from the UK, which link several British airports to Corfu (around 3 hours flight time).

The only regularly scheduled flights to Corfu on commercial carriers depart from Athens (45 minutes). If you are traveling from North America, you might find it just as cheap to fly to London and pick up a charter flight.

GUIDES and TOURS *(xenagós; periodía)*

Authorized multilingual guide-interpreters work through hotels and travel agencies. Contact the E.O.T. office or the Association of Corfu Travel Agents (see tourist information)

Among the numerous tours offered are those to Paleokastrítsa, the Achílleion, and Corfu Town, as well as Greek Nights, boat trips, and day trips to Paxos and mainland Greece. You can book these and other tours through travel agents.

We'd like an English-speaking guide.	**Tha thélame éna xenagó pou milái anglká.**

HEALTH and MEDICAL CARE

In theory, EU citizens with an E111 form (obtainable in their own country) can get free treatment under the Greek health service. However, you are likely to receive the minimum treatment, and state hospital facilities are over-stretched in the tourist season. It's therefore essential to obtain private medical insurance for your holiday.

Doctors and dentists are concentrated in Corfu Town; your hotel or studio owner will be able to find you one who speaks English. Most resorts have a local medical office, with hours and telephone numbers posted.

Hospitals. The capital's hospital and clinics operate a 24-hour emergency service (Tel. 166, or 0661 39403) that dispatches ambulances to any point on the island with admirable speed. Otherwise, call the all-purpose emergency number **100** or the tourist police (Tel. 0661 30265). Corfu General Hospital is situated on Policroníou Konstantá Street in Corfu Town (seven phone lines: Tel. 0661 45811/7). Corfu Private General Clinic is located on the main Paleokastrítsa Road, just outside Corfu Town center (Tel. 0661 36044 or 0661 22946).

Corfu

Pharmacies (ΦΑΡΜΑΚΕΙΟ — *farmakío*). A red or green cross on a white background identifies a pharmacy (chemist). They are open during normal shop hours, and a notice on the door should tell you the nearest one for after-hours service. One pharmacy is always open in Corfu Town at night and on Saturday and Sunday. Without a prescription, you can't get sleeping pills, barbiturates, or medicine for stomach upsets.

Mosquitoes (nonmalarial) can be a nuisance on Corfu, so bring along mosquito repellent. Or you can buy small electric devices that you plug in at night to keep the bugs at bay.

a doctor/a dentist	**énas giatrós/ énas odontogiatrós**
hospital	**nosokomío**
an upset stomach	**varistomachiá**
sunstroke	**ilíasi**
a fever	**piretós**

HOLIDAYS *(argíes)*

Banks, offices, and shops are closed on the following national holidays, as well as during some feasts and festivals (see Calendar of Events, page 84):

1 January	*Protochroniá*	New Year's Day
6 January	*ton Theofaníon*	Epiphany
25 March	*Ikostí Pémti Martíou (tou Evangelismoú)*	Greek Independence Day
1 May	*Protomagiá*	May Day
15 August	*Dekapendávgoustos (tis Panagías)*	Assumption Day

28 October	*Ikostí Ogdóï Oktovríou*	Òchi ("No") Day,
	celebrating defiance of Italian ultimatum and invasion of 1940	
25 December	*Christoúgenna*	Christmas Day
26 December	*Défteri Iméra ton Christougénnon*	St. Stephen's Day

Moveable dates:

Katharí Deftéra	1st Day of Lent: Clean Monday
Megáli Paraskeví	Good Friday
Deftéra tou Páscha	Easter Monday
tou Agíou Pnévmatos	Whit Monday ("Holy Spirit"), usually in June

Note: The moveable holidays are celebrated according to dates in the Greek Orthodox calendar, which often differ from Catholic or Protestant dates.

LANGUAGE

Only in remote countryside spots will non-Greek-speaking tourists run into serious communication problems. You will find that basic English is spoken almost everywhere, as are Italian, German, and French, to some degree.

Stress is a very important feature of the Greek language, denoted by an accent above the vowel of the syllable to be emphasized.

The table below lists the Greek letters in their upper- and lower-case forms, followed by the letters to which they correspond in the English language.

Corfu

A	α	a	as in *bar*
B	β	v	
Γ	γ	g	as in *go**
Δ	δ	d	like **th** in *this*
E	ε	e	as in *get*
Z	ζ	z	
H	η	i	like **ee** in *meet*
Θ	θ	th	as in *thin*
I	ι	i	like **ee** in *meet*
K	κ	k	
Λ	λ	l	
M	μ	m	
N	v	n	
Ξ	ξ	x	like **ks** in *thanks*
O	o	o	as in *got*
Π	π	p	
P	ρ	r	
Σ	σ, ς	s	as in *kiss*
T	τ	t	
Y	υ	i	like **ee** in *meet*
Φ	φ	f	
X	χ	ch	as in Scottish *loch*
Ψ	ψ	ps	as in *tipsy*
<u>O</u>/Ω	ω	o	as in *got*
OY	ου	oo/ou	as in *soup*

*except before "i" and "e" sounds, when it's pronounced like the *y* in *yes*.

You'll find a list of useful expressions inside the cover of this guide, and the *Berlitz Greek Phrase Book and Dictionary* covers practically all the situations you're likely to encounter in your travels.

M

MEDIA

Newspapers and magazines (*efimerída*; *periodikó*). During the tourist season, foreign-language newspapers are on sale at shops and kiosks on the island, generally on the day after publication. The only local English-language publication is *The Corfiote*. Although aimed largely at the ex-pat market, it's still a good read for vacationers, with such useful information as restaurant reviews and bus schedules. Outside of Corfu Town, however, it is difficult to find.

Television (*tileórasi*). Most hotels and many bars offer satellite television networks, including CNN and Sky.

Radio. BBC World Service is broadcast on the short-wave band (try 15.07 MHz and 12.09 MHz), but reception is poor.

MONEY

Currency (*nómisma*). Greece's monetary unit is the drachma (in Greek; *drachmi* ΔΡΑΧΜΕΣ). In the plural, it is abbreviated *drs.* (and colloquially called "drax").

Coins. 5, 10, 20, 50, 100 drs.

Banknotes: 100, 500, 1,000, 5,000, 10,000 drs.

Banks and currency exchange (ΤΡΑΠΠΕΖΑ — *trápeza*; ΣΥΝΑΛΛΑΓΜΑ — *sinállagma*). You'll find banks in Corfu Town and in the larger resort areas. Hotels and travel agencies (the latter sometimes called "tourist offices") are authorized to change money, but you will probably get less for your money than you would from a bank. You can also exchange money at post offices, at a better rate than at the aforementioned places. You'll need your passport as identification to change traveler's checks (but not to change cash).

ATMs. The easiest method to obtain cash is through an ATM "hole-in-the-wall" dispenser. These can be found in Corfu Town and in some of the larger resorts. Depending upon your own individual card fees, this might also be the cheapest way to get money.

Credit cards (*pistotikí kárta*). Internationally known credit cards are accepted in many shops (indicated by a sign in the window) and at car rental firms, most hotels, more expensive restaurants, and some (but not all) filling stations. Be aware that you might have to pay an additional five to seven percent for the privilege of using plastic.

Traveler's checks. Most major brands of traveler's checks — in any Western currency — are readily cashed. Always take your passport for identification. Eurocheques are sometimes accepted.

I want to change some pounds/dollars.	**Thélo na alláxo merikés líres/meriká dollária.**
traveler's checks	**taxidiotikés epitagés**
Can I pay with this credit card?	**Boró na pliróso me aftí ti pistotikí kárta?**

OPENING HOURS

The siesta (the traditional Mediterranean lunchtime break) is still alive and well in Corfu, observed more strictly outside tourist areas.

Shops. Traditional hours are generally Monday to Saturday from 8:30am or 9am until 1:30pm or 2pm. On Tuesday, Thursday, and Friday shops reopen in the evening from 5pm until 8:30pm or 9pm. Shops catering to tourists often stay open through the siesta and until late each evening in the summer. Larger supermarkets open Monday to Saturday from 8am to 9pm and Sunday from 9am to 2pm or even later.

Museums and tourist attractions. Hours vary greatly, but it is worth noting that Corfu Town's three main state-run museums are closed on Monday. They are open Tuesday through Saturday from 8:30am to 3pm and Sunday from 8:30am or 9:30am to 2:30pm or 3pm.

Banks. Monday to Friday from 8am or 8:30am to 1:30pm or 2pm.

Post offices. Monday to Friday from 7:30am to 2pm (the main post office in Corfu Town closes at 8pm and is open Saturday mornings in July and August).

Businesses and offices. 8am to 1pm, then 2pm to 4pm.

Restaurants and tavernas. More traditional establishments open for lunch from noon until around 3pm and for dinner from 7pm to around 11pm. More tourist-oriented establishments might open early for breakfast or coffee and stay open throughout the day.

POLICE (ΑΣΤΥΝΟΜΙΑ — *astinomía*)

Emergency telephone number: **100**

Tourist police: 0661 30265.

The Tourist Police (*touristikí astinomía*) has a specific mission to help visitors to the island, as well as to accompany state inspectors to hotels and restaurants to ensure that proper standards and prices are maintained.

If you need to report a loss or theft to the police, go to the police station closest to the scene of the crime. Each group of villages has a police station — you'll have to ask its location and go there.

Traffic police check car documents, operate speed traps, and issue fines for illegal parking (fines in Greece are high).

Where's the nearest police station?	**Pou íne to kodinótero astinomikó tmíma?**

POST OFFICES (ΤΑΧΥΔΡΟΜΕΙΟ — *tachidromío*)

Post offices handle letters, parcels, money orders, and foreign currency exchange. They also sell stamps. Look for a yellow OTE sign with a post-horn logo. (You cannot make phone calls from post offices here.)

Post offices are generally open Monday to Friday from 8am to 2pm. The main post office is in Corfu Town, at the corner of Alexándras and Megális (Tel. 0661 25544). It is open Monday to Friday from 7:30am to 8pm (until 2:30pm for money orders and parcels) and Saturday mornings in July and August. Registered letters and parcels to foreign destinations are checked before being sent, so don't seal them until presenting them at the desk.

Stamps are also sold at most shops and hotels selling postcards. Stamps for a postcard to Europe cost 170 drs.; those to places farther afield cost 200 drs. Delivery to Europe takes about five to seven days.

Letter boxes are yellow. In tourist hotels, the receptionist will take care of dispatching your mail.

Have you received any mail for…?	**échete grámmata giá…?**

A stamp for this letter/postcard, please.	**éna grammatósimo giaftó to grámma/giaftí tin kart postál, parakaló.**
express (special delivery)	**exprés**
airmail	**aeroporikós**
registered	**sistiméno**

PUBLIC TRANSPORTATION

Buses (*leoforío*). The island's public bus service is not always efficient, but it is a good value. Timetables are displayed at bus stops (ΣΤΑΣΙΣ — *stásis*) in the capital. They are also available from the tourist office in Corfu Town and in *The Corfiote*. There are no all-night bus services.

There are two types of buses on the island. The blue town buses serve towns and villages in the vicinity of Corfu Town, including Kontokáli, Gouviá, Dassiá, the Achílleion, and Pélekas. Buses for Kanóni depart from near the Esplanade. All other blue buses leave from San Rocco Square (Tel. 0661 31595). Country buses are green and cream-colored; they leave from the coach station on Avriamou Street, by the New Fort (Tel. 0661 30627, 0661 39985, or 0661 39862).

For all buses, buy your tickets on board or from kiosks in the square. You can flag a bus down anywhere within reason; it will also drop you off between stops if it is not inconvenient.

What's the fare to… ?	**Piá íne i timí giá… ?**
When's the next bus to… ?	**Póte févgi to epómeno leoforío giá… ?**
single (one-way)/ return (round-trip)	**apló/me epistrofí**

Corfu

Taxis (ΤΑΞΙ — *taxí*). Taxis are based in Corfu Town (blue ones) and in the country (gray). Taxi ranks in town are at the New Port, Old Port, Spilia, Esplanade, Pallas Cinema, and San Rocco Square. There are two rates on the meter: a slow one used in Corfu Town and on two-way journeys, and a fast rate for single out-of-town trips (the meter is changed from "slow" to "fast" at the town boundary). Check the fare before you get in the cab; if the meter is mysteriously "broken," you will have to agree on a fare with the driver. Radio taxis can be called (Tel. 0661 33811/2), for which there's a small surcharge.

Ferries. Regular ferries run to the Ionian islands of Paxos and Cephalonia. The Ionians are not a group for island-hopping, however. It takes three hours just to sail to Paxos and nine hours to Cephalonia. To get to any other islands requires changing on the mainland.

Ferries also go to Pátra, Athens, and Thessalonika on the Greek mainland and to various ports in Italy. All depart from Corfu Town, though there is an additional service to Igoumenítsa from Lefkímmi (near Kávos).

For current ferry schedules and fares, check with your nearest travel agent.

What's the fare to…?   **Piá íne i timí giá… ?**

R

RELIGION

The national religion of Greece is the Greek Orthodox Church. You must dress modestly to visit both churches and monasteries, which normally means long trousers for men, a long skirt for women, and covered shoulders for both sexes. Men might be allowed to wear long shorts, and skirts might be provided for women to wrap around themselves.

T

TELEPHONE *(tiléfono)*

Local calling. There are two codes on the island for calls within Corfu. For calls to Corfu Town and the south, use the prefix **0661**. For calls to the north, northeast, and west, use the prefix **0663**. The code for the island of Paxos is **0662**.

From overseas. To call Corfu from abroad, first dial the international access code (00 from the UK, 011 from North America), then **30** (the country code for Greece). Add the local area code for Corfu — **661** or **663** (without the 0; see above) — before dialing the number itself.

Long distance from Corfu. International direct dialing is available at street corner phones. These take phonecards, which are by far the easiest and cheapest way to phone home. International trunk lines are often busy and might require a long wait at peak times. To reverse charges (collect calls), dial 151 for Europe and 161 for the rest of the world.
   In higher-grade hotels you can dial long distance from your room, but charges can be exorbitant. Standard rates are available from the international operator (dial 161). For the local operator, dial 132.

Coin phones. These accept 10-, 20-, and 50-drachma coins. Phonecards can be bought at kiosks and hotels.

Fax and Internet service. Fax services are available at major hotels, post offices, and some travel agencies. There is an Internet café in Corfu Town: Planet Cyber Café, at 40 Alexandras Street.

reverse-charge (collect) call   **plirotéo apó to paralípti**

Corfu

TIME ZONES

Greek time is GMT + 2. The chart below shows the times in Corfu and various other cities in summer (when Greek clocks are put forward one hour, as in many other parts of the world).

New York	London	**Corfu**	Jo'burg	Sydney	Auckland
5am	10am	**noon**	11am	7pm	9pm

TIPPING

By law, a tax (VAT) is added to the bill at hotels, restaurants, and tavernas. The Greeks aren't tip-crazy, but it is the norm to leave a little more if service has been good.

Hotel porter	200 drs. per bag
Hotel maid	500 drs. per day
Waiter	5 percent–10 percent
Taxi driver	10 percent
Tour guide	500 drs.–1,000 drs. per day
Hairdresser/barber	10 percent
Lavatory attendant	50 drs.

TOILETS (toualéttes)

Public conveniences are best avoided. But if you are desperate in Corfu Town, there are toilets at the following locations: Plateía G Theotóki, near the Esplanade bandstand (on Kapodístrias Street on the southern part of the Esplanade), opposite Barclays Bank in San Rocco Square, and at the square in the Old Port. Take along your own toilet paper. Leave a small tip if there's someone in attendance.

A better option is to use facilities at museums or the better cafés. If you do drop in specifically to use the toilet, it's customary to purchase coffee or some other drink before leaving.

Note: You are always expected to put toilet tissue in the waste bin rather than down the toilet. Due to their narrow-bore pipes, toilets easily become clogged.

Where are the toilets?   **Pou íne i toualéttes?**

TOURIST INFORMATION (*grafío pliroforión tourismoú*)

The Greek National Tourist Organization (*Ellinikós Organismós Tourismoú*, abbreviated E.O.T.) has the following offices abroad:

Australia: 51–57 Pitt Street, Sydney, NSW 2000;
Tel. (02) 9241 1663.

Canada: 1300 Bay Street, Toronto, Ontario M5R 3K8; Tel. (416) 968 2220; 1233 rue de la Montagne, Montreal, Quebec H3G 1Z2; Tel. (514) 871 1535.

UK: 4 Conduit Street, London W1R 0DJ; Tel. 0207 734 5997.

US: 645 Fifth Avenue, New York, NY 10022; Tel. (212) 421 5777.

These offices supply general information and glossy pictures, but when it comes to anything specific on Corfu they are usually of little help.

There is only one office in Corfu, tucked out of the way at the corner of Rizospaston Voulefton Street and Polila Street on K Zavistanou Street. It is open 8am–2:15pm from Monday to Friday (Tel. 0661 37520, 0661 37639, 0661 37640; fax 0661 30298). There is very little information to take away, and the quality of assistance depends very much on who assists you.

It is much easier to get local information from a travel agency (some of these actually call themselves "tourist offices"). But you should remember that their information might not be impartial, as they have a vested interest in selling you excursions or at least in

Corfu

pointing you in certain directions. One agency, however, that can be thoroughly recommended to vacationers in the northeast of the island is the Travel Shop, in Kassiópi (Tel. 0663 81220).

Where's the tourist office?   **Pou íne to grafío tourismoú?**

Planning your trip on the Web: Many local Corfu travel agencies and hotels have their own Web sites, but these vary greatly in quality. A typical one is <www.corfuxenos.gr>. Use your browser and enter the words *Corfu travel* to locate these and other sites. The official Greek National Tourist office Web site is <www.antor.com/Greece/index.html>. It has little on Corfu but is worth a browse.

W

WEIGHTS and MEASURES

Length

Weight

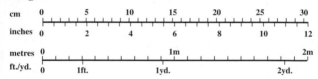

Temperature

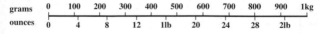

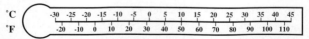

Recommended Hotels

Most hotels in Corfu get booked up quickly for the high season: from mid-June until October and, in particular, around the middle of August. Make sure that you reserve well ahead (see ACCOMMODATIONS, page 102). To phone a hotel, dial the international country code for Greece (30), followed by the Corfu code and number provided in our listings.

All hotels are classified by the Greek National Tourist Organization: luxury (L) class is at the very top, then A class down to E class (only hotels of L, A, B, and C classes are featured below). This class rating establishes minimum price rates, but prices can often vary widely within each class according to the season, location, and availability of rooms. By law, rates must always be posted in all rooms.

The price categories below are for a double room with bath (but without breakfast) in high season. All hotel room rates include VAT (Value Added Tax) of 18 percent. All listed hotels accept credit cards. Luxury hotels (L class) all have air-conditioning; unless otherwise noted, it should be assumed that any other listed hotel does not have air-conditioning. Many hotels on the island are open only from April to October. Those on Corfu Town are open all year round

$	under 10,000 drs.
$$	10,000–15,000 drs.
$$$	16,000–30,000 drs.
$$$$	above 30,000 drs.

Corfu Town

Archontico $–$$ *Athanassíou 61, Garítsa; Tel. 0661 37222; fax 0661 36950. C class.* This converted mansion lies a 15–20 minute walk south of the Esplanade along the seafront. It has a nicely old-fashioned ambiance but offers a variety of modern amenities plus a pleasant garden café and bar. Note that there is some traffic noise at the front. 29 rooms.

Arkadion $ *Kapodistríou St., Corfu Town; Tel. 0661 37670; fax 0661 45087. C class.* Rooms are somewhat small and there is a lot of street noise, but you can't beat the location — right on the Esplanade at the southern end of the Listón. Balconies look right down into café-goers' coffee cups. The staff here are friendly, and this hotel offers good value for its location. 95 rooms.

Bella Venezia $$ *N. Zambéli 4, Corfu Town; Tel. 0661 44290; fax 0661 20708. B class .* Corfu Town's worst-kept secret, this modern hotel is in a lovely, renovated neoclassical Venetian building right in the center of town. It's very popular with both Greek and foreign visitors. Excellent lobby and bar area plus an attractive garden terrace. Good staff and great value for the location. 32 rooms.

Cavalieri $$$ *Kapodistríou St. 4, Corfu Town; Tel. 0661 39041; fax 0661 39283. A class .* This converted six-story 17th-century French nobleman's mansion, set at the end of the Esplanade, is a charming and comfortable place to stay in the center of town. Worth a visit even if you are not staying here just to see its roof garden's great views. Rooms are air-conditioned. 50 rooms.

Corfu Palace Hotel $$$$ *Leofóros Democratías 2, Corfu Town; Tel. 0661 39485; fax 0661 31749. L class* All rooms have a sea view in this graceful luxury hotel overlooking Garítsa Bay, just a ten-minute walk south of the Esplanade. Its beautiful grounds, featuring expansive lawns and subtropical gardens, border the old Venetian city walls. The hotel's many amenities include indoor and outdoor swimming pools, two restaurants, and two bars. 115 rooms.

The South

Apollo Palace $$$ *Messongí; Tel. 0661 55433; fax. 0661 55602. Class A* . This attractive, modern, well-run hotel complex is set 100 m (330 ft) from the beach. It has its own gardens, pool, tennis, restaurant, and bar. Rooms are air-conditioned. 251 rooms.

Corfu Holiday Palace $$$$ *Nafsikás Street, Kanóni; Tel. 0661 36540; fax. 0661 36551. Class L.* Formerly the Hilton, this long-established deluxe hotel is set on a peninsula in lovely grounds, featuring the famous view of Mouse Island. Inside it is a large, older-style property with traditional furnishings, some stylish, some a little aged. It has its own secluded sandy beach plus two pools, tennis, ten-pin bowling lanes, health club facilities, restaurants, bars, and the island's only casino. 209 rooms, 37 bungalows.

Delfinia $$$ *Moraḯtika. Tel. 0661 76320; fax. 0661 75450; e-mail: <delfinia@hotel.gr>. Class A* . Set next to a private beach in a shady olive grove with lemon trees and gardens of subtropical plants. All rooms have balconies. Facilities include a swimming pool, tennis courts, beach bars, fitness club, and watersports. 86 rooms.

Golden Sands $$ *Ágios Georgiós; Tel. 0661 51225; fax 0661 51140. Class B.* Attractive low-rise hotel with a stylish interior set close to the main sandy beach, across the road from a small rocky cliff. The grounds feature small, well-kept lawns and a pool. 78 rooms.

Corfu

Messonghi Beach $$ *Moraítika; Tel. 0661 76684; fax. 0661 75334. Class B.* By far the largest complex on the island, the Messonghi Beach, renovated in 1997, is almost a village in itself. Its adequate, simple accommodations are set in semi-detached bungalows or the 6-story main block. All rooms have a balcony or terrace. The grounds comprise extensive lawns with palm trees and include 4 pools, cafés, bars, discos, shops, watersports, scuba diving, tennis center, fitness center, and a good children's playground. 920 rooms.

San Stéfano $$$–$$$$ *Benítses; Tel. 0661 71112; fax. 0661 71124. Class A.* This modern, white hotel enjoys a wonderful site high on the hillside, next to the Achílleion Palace and above Benítses. Set in 14 hectares (35 acres) of private gardens, it was specially revamped as one of the host hotels for the 1994 EEC summit, so rooms are excellent and include air-conditioning. Facilities include the largest swimming pool on Corfu, sun terraces, shops, children's playground, and tennis courts. 259 rooms.

North of Corfu Town

Chandris Hotels $$$ *Dassiá Bay; Tel. 0661 97100; fax 0661 93458; e-mail: <chandris@ath.forthnet.gr>. A class.* Chandris operates two large, well-maintained hotels — the Corfu Chandris and the Dassiá Chandris — side by side on Dassiá Bay, separated from the sea by large private gardens. Rooms are in the main buildings, bungalows, or chalets. Ask for a seaview to avoid a road-facing room. Facilities include air-conditioning, swimming pool, tennis, restaurants, and children's club. Corfu Chandris 301 rooms; Dassiá Chandris 251 rooms. Both have wheelchair access.

Dassiá Beach Hotel $$ *Dassiá; Tel./fax 0661 93224. C class.* Situated right beside the beach, away from the busy main road, the rooms here all have balconies, some overlooking the sea. The grounds are attractive and there is a very nice bar and restaurant terrace. 54 rooms.

Corfu Imperial $$$$ *Kommeno; Tel. 0661 91481; fax. 0661 91881. L class.* Set on its own secluded private peninsula with man-made sandy cove beaches, this luxurious hotel successfully mixes contemporary and classic elements and was one of the hosts of the 1994 EEC summit. The stylish Imperial is a resort in itself, with a huge seawater swimming pool, a wide range of watersports, choice of restaurants and bars, a tennis club, health club, and shops. Rooms are nicely furnished and are either in the main block or in bungalows dotted around the pretty grounds. 304 rooms.

Daphnilia Bay $$$ *Daphnilia; Tel. 0661 90320; fax 0661 91026. A class.* Set 1 km (0.6 mile) from Dassiá in superb gardens, the Daphnilia Bay offers a very high standard of accommodation either in attractive bungalows or the 4-story main block. The beach is 300 m (980 ft) down a large slope. Facilities include a good-sized pool, tennis court, playground, and watersports. 260 rooms.

Kondokáli Bay Hotel $$$$ *Kondokáli; Tel. 0661 99000; fax 0661 91901. L class.* This modern, low-rise bungalow-style hotel boasts beautiful gardens next to a private sandy beach. Deluxe rooms are very well equipped. Facilities include a swimming pool, restaurant, beach bar, health club, tennis courts, watersports, and an imaginative children's club. 152 rooms, 81 bungalows.

Corfu

Louis Corcyra Beach Hotel $$$ *Gouviá; Tel. 0661 90196; fax 0661 91591. A class.* This pleasant hotel-bungalow complex is right in the heart of the Gouviá resort but tucked away among well-tended lawns and gardens that slope down to a narrow, compacted-sand beach. Bedrooms and public areas are modern, stylish, and well maintained. Air-conditioning is available in all rooms. Facilities include a pool, tennis courts, squash court, children's club, and playground. 260 rooms.

The Northeast

Nautilus Hotel $ *Barbáti; Tel. 0661 93620; fax 0661 93870. C class.* These simply furnished rooms housed in three two-story blocks enjoy a great location perched high above Barbáti. Swimming pool and restaurant; the nearest tavernas are a 10-minute walk. 64 rooms.

The White House $$ *Kalámi; available only through CV Travel (Tel. in the UK: 0870 606 0013).* The ground floor of the famous White House, where Lawrence Durrell wrote *Prospero's Cell,* is now a taverna. The upstairs has been converted to a self-catering holiday home sleeping 4–8 people. Accommodation is comfortable, spacious, and airy, with the original dining table and desk that Durrell used. The location (at the very end of the road in Kalámi) and views — across the bay and beach and out to Albania — are splendid. 4 rooms.

The North and Northwest

Ionian Princess Hotel $$ *Acharávi; Tel. 0663 63110; fax. 0663 63111. B class.* Built in the traditional Greek-villa style, this large modern hotel (renovated in 1997) is a five-minute walk from the beach and has a restaurant, a taverna, two swimming pools, gardens, tennis, and a children's club. Apartments are also available. 154 rooms.

Hotel Róda Beach $$ *Róda; Tel. 0663 63202. B class.* This was Róda's first hotel, last renovated in 1997. It is rather secluded from the town, with extensive gardens that lead down to the beach. It includes three swimming pools (one for children), tennis, a basic fitness room, restaurants, and bar. 393 rooms. Wheelchair access (partial).

Sellas Hotel $–$$ *Sidári; Tel. 0663 95285; fax 0663 95311. C class.* This quiet family-run hotel, popular with British visitors (can be crowded in high season), is located ten minutes away from the town center and five minutes from the Canal d'Amour. Rooms are spacious and simply furnished, with balcony. Facilities include swimming pool, restaurant, and bars. All-inclusive package available. 44 rooms.

Silver Beach Hotel $–$$ *Róda; Tel. 0663 63112; fax 0663 63076. C class.* Small and relaxed, this family-run hotel is located three minutes from the beach and has a pool, restaurant, bar and large gardens. 33 rooms.

The West

Akrotiri Beach Hotel $$$ *Paleokastrítsa; Tel. 0663 41275/winter 0661 46500; fax. 0663 41277/winter 0661 20708; e-mail: <belvenht@hol.gr>. A class.* This modern 5-story resort hotel, renovated in 1997, stands on a headland overlooking the sea and offers high quality air-conditioned rooms, all with verandas looking onto the sea. Facilities include two swimming pools, tennis courts, restaurants, bars, and shops. 127 rooms.

Corfu

Ermónes Beach Hotel $$–$$$ *Ermónes; Tel. 0661 94241, fax: 0661 94248. A class.* This bungalow-style hotel enjoys a spectacular setting as it spills down hillside terraces high above Ermónes Bay. Its three levels are linked by a funicular-style lift to a restaurant and pool above and beach below. A good choice for sporty types, with tennis and watersports available and Corfu's golf course just five minutes away by car. All rooms have excellent views; the hotel is cleverly designed so that other rooms are out of sight, even when you are on your own balcony. 272 rooms.

Glyfáda Beach Hotel $$ *Glyfáda; Tel. 0661 94258; fax 0661 94257. B class.* This plain and simple 3-story hotel is ideal for a quiet, relaxing beach holiday. Rooms are of good size, with balconies facing the sea. There are two tavernas nearby. 35 rooms.

Grand Hotel Glyfáda Beach $$$ *Glyfáda; Tel. 0661 94141; fax 0661 94146. A class.* This outstanding property, right on Glyfáda Beach, is one of the island's best hotels. The furnishings are sumptuous and the décor is a tasteful mix of antique and modern furniture. Facilities include a pool, small lawn and playground, two restaurants, bar, disco and live music, and watersports. 242 rooms.

Paxos

Paxos Club Apartments Hotel $$–$$$ *Gaios; Tel. 0662 32450; fax. 0662 32097. B class.* Set in an olive grove 2 km (1.2 miles) outside Gaios Town, this stylish small hotel has been sensitively built around a century-old traditional island house, which is now used as the restaurant (the food is excellent). There's a lovely pool in front; a Jacuzzi, piano bar, and children's playground. All rooms are spacious and air-conditioned with a kitchenette and a balcony or patio. Book well ahead for high season. 23 apartments.

Recommended Restaurants

Restaurants in resort areas are typically open only during the high season (mid-June to October). Those in Corfu Town are open year round.

Unless otherwise indicated, traditional establishments generally open for lunch from noon until around 3pm and for dinner from 7pm to around 11pm. More tourist-oriented establishments might open early for breakfast or coffee and stay open throughout the day.

Specific times and days of closing below are for summer season, so if you are planning a special journey to dine during low season, it's always advisable to call to confirm. Reservations are necessary only at top restaurants in high season or on Sunday at lunchtime, when Corfiote families eat out en masse. If a telephone number is not provided, it is because reservations are not taken. A typical taverna will usually bring out more tables and chairs rather than turn you away!

The following prices reflect the average cost of a two-course meal (per person) and a half bottle of wine. The most expensive restaurants add a service charge to your bill (usually around ten percent), but the vast majority of restaurants do not. At all restaurants, however, an automatic tax of 18 percent (VAT) is always included in the prices listed on the menu. It is customary to leave an additional five to ten percent for the waiter.

$	under 3,000 drs.
$$	3,000–6,000 drs.
$$$	over 6,000 drs.

Corfu Town

Aegli $$ *Kapodistriou 23; Tel. 0661 31949.* Open daily all day. This smart, long-established restaurant faces the Listón (with tables also on Kapodistríou Street) and offers a good range of typical Corfiote cooking and international dishes to suit all budgets and tastes. Start with aubergine (eggplant) croquettes and cheese rolls, then go for the rooster stew, whitefish *(bourdéto),* or lamb with vegetables. Quick and efficient service. Major credit cards.

Albatros $$$ *Corfu Palace Hotel, Leofóros Democratías 2; Tel. 0661 39485.* Open daily for lunch and dinner. For a special treat, sample the international and local specialties served in the distinguished grillroom of the Corfu Palace Hotel. Live music is also provided. Major credit cards.

Art Gallery Café $ *Palace of St Michael and St George, East Wing, off Esplanade; no reservations.* Open daily all day. Tucked away behind the Palace of St. Michael and St. George, next to the Municipal Art Gallery, these quiet tea gardens are set on a delightful terrace with seaviews. It is the perfect place to rest a while from museum, gallery, and fort sightseeing or to start an evening out. Drinks and snacks (excellent cappuccino) but not full meals. Art exhibitions are also held here. Cash only.

Averof $–$$ *Prosaléndiou 4; Tel. 0661 31468.* Open daily for lunch and dinner. This busy restaurant, well known to locals and tourists alike, is situated down a narrow street a little way in from the Old Port. There is a wide selection of local dishes to be sampled, as well as a variety of Corfiote house wines. Cash only.

Chrissomállis $ *N. Theotóki 6; Tel. 0661 30342.* Open daily all day. This simple taverna and grill room just off the Listón serves a selection of grilled meats and Greek specialties, including *pastitsáda, sofríto* (beef or veal stew), and *moussaká.* Cash only.

Cofineta $$–$$$ *Kapodistríou 96; Tel. 0661 25642.* Open daily 10am–midnight. Restaurant and bar in a splendid location near the palace at the top of the Listón. Tables are arranged around a lovely flower garden. There is an Italian and Continental menu with some Greek dishes also available. Scrumptious selection of ice cream sundaes. Cash only.

Corfu Pizza $ *Kapodistríou 6; Tel. 0661 35976.* Open daily noon–midnight. Located close to the bandstand on the Esplanade, this is the place to come for the best pizza in town. There is also an interesting selection of Greek specialties.

Faliraki $$$ *Murayia, St. Nicholas Gate; Tel. 0661 30392.* Open daily for lunch and dinner. This famous, long-established eating house enjoys a superb position on a small promontory with views of Albania, Vídos Island, and the Old Fort. It serves excellent Greek food with modern international touches and is renowned for its seafood specials. Major credit cards.

Olympia Café $ *Listón 24.* Open daily all day. This splendid café under the arches still retains its original French period décor, with green marble tabletops, mahogany-paneled mirrors, and an array of sculpted wood ceiling decorations. This is a good spot for coffee and a snack rather than a full meal. Cash only.

Oréstes $$–$$$ *Xen. Stratigoú 78; Tel. 0661 35664.* Open daily for lunch and dinner. This highly regarded seafood restaurant is appropriately situated near the New Port. Pleasant outdoor dining area. Major credit cards.

Rex $$–$$$ *Kapodistríou 66; Tel. 0661 39649.* Open all day daily. Established in 1932, the Rex is something of a Corfu Town institution. It serves a wide range of Corfiote, Greek, and northern European cuisine. Major credit cards.

Corfu

Tenedos $$ *Solomou Street; Tel. 0661 36277.* Open daily from 9am until late. Charming little restaurant on the steps leading to the New Fort, this informal alfresco spot is right by the bright-pink landmark Tenedos Church. The owners are French and Greek; perhaps not surprisingly, the food is a mix of international and local dishes. Leave room for a delicious homemade fruit pie. Live music nightly; half-price meals for children. Major credit cards.

Venetian Well Bistrot $$$ *Plateía Kremastí; Tel. 0661 44761.* Open daily 7pm–11pm; closed Sundays in winter. Hidden away in the maze-like Old Town, the Venetian Well enjoys probably the loveliest setting in all Corfu Town and serves some of the best food, too. Dine to the soothing strains of classical music, either outside around a 17th-century Venetian wellhead or inside the beautifully restored house. The imaginative menu changes every day, featuring mostly international dishes (such as wild boar, duck in kumquat sauce, or chicken in champagne) but with plenty of Greek choices as well. Service is attentive, and there is a superb wine list. Major credit cards.

Xeníkhtis $$$ *Potamoú 12; Tel. 0661 24911.* Open daily for lunch and dinner; closed Sundays. Situated on the main road north, just outside the town center, this highly acclaimed restaurant offers Greek, French, and Italian cuisine. As an example of its attention to detail, fresh Norwegian salmon is delivered almost daily on the Oslo–Corfu flight. There is a nice intimate atmosphere, with occasional live music. Major credit cards.

Yisdhákis $ *Solomoú 20; Tel. 0661 37578.* Open daily noon–11pm. The lower end of Solomoú Street is a good place to come for authentic Greek cooking on a budget. Make your choice from a variety of daily specials, all simmering under the glass counter. Cash only.

The South

Taverna Trípa $$$ *Kinopiástes; Tel. 0661 56333.* Open daily for lunch and dinner. This marvelous 50-year old taverna is an award-winning Corfu institution (7 km/4 miles southwest of Corfu Town). Countless celebrities and heads of state have come here and continue to do so. Dining is on a large vine-covered patio. There is an array of delectable appetizers, followed by such choices as spit-roasted lamb or pheasant. Fine selection of desserts and wine. Greek music and folk dancing take place most nights. Major credit cards.

Captain's $$ *Kanoní (just after Mouse Island viewpoint); Tel. 0661 40502.* Open daily all day. Touristy it might be, but Captain George's homemade Greek specials have delighted many a Kanoní daytripper. Don't miss the unusual dip of *kopanisti* (cheese and hot pepper pounded together) as a starter, then move onto kebabs or *pastitsáda*. The atmosphere is very lively, and there is a small playground area for children. Major credit cards.

Memories Taverna $$ *Messongi (south end of beach); Tel. 0661 75283.* Open daily for lunch and dinner. Set in a quieter part of this busy resort, Memories is memorable for its authentic Corfiote cooking and wine from the barrel. Major credit cards.

North of Corfu Town

Gerékos $$–$$$ *Kondokáli Village; Tel. 0661 91281.* Open daily noon–11pm. Whether you dine at the original fish taverna or its sister restaurant (which goes under the same name) across the road, service is friendly and the fish exquisitely prepared. For a particularly tasty starter, try the *bouillabaisse*. The house white wine is recommended. Major credit cards.

Corfu

Taverna Greco $$$ *Dafnilia (Dassiá–Tzavros road); Tel. 0661 91765.* Open daily noon–1am. If your palate is a little jaded from one too many lukewarm *moussakás,* try the New Greek cooking at this smart but friendly taverna with classic Greek blue-and-white décor. All food is homemade, and the menu features some unusual dishes. Start with homemade *dolmádes,* then try one of the house specialty pies, perhaps accompanied by the excellent *gemista* (stuffed vegetables). Greek dancing every night. Major credit cards.

The Northeast

Agni Taverna $$ *Agni; Tel. 0663 91142.* Open daily for lunch and dinner. Many accolades have already been heaped on this lovely 120-year-old taverna. The setting — a spotless white pebble beach, crystal blue waters, and a handful of colorful caiques — is perfection. The lively young proprietors are an Anglo-Greek team, and the food reflects this. It's Greek with a modern international twist: boned sardines stuffed with cheese, mussels in wine and herbs, lamb in red wine. Don't drive to any of Agni's three restaurants. Instead, come by the special boats from Kalámi. Major credit cards.

Galini Taverna $$–$$$ *Ágios Stéfanos; Tel. 0663 81492.* Open daily for lunch and dinner. Enjoy a perfect front-row seat for the picture-postcard bay of Ágios Stéfanos. This very highly rated taverna has been serving traditional Greek food since 1963. Major credit cards.

Taverna Nikolas $$ *Agni; Tel. 0663 91243.* Open daily for lunch and dinner. Pericles, the ebullient current owner, is carrying on a century-old family tradition of Corfiote village cooking. Try the *arní lemonato* (village-style lemon-herbed lamb), *sikóti krasato* (liver and onions in wine), or *koukouyerios* (fried cod with garlic sauce). One of the best Greek Nights on the island happens here every Thursday, starring Pericles and his athletic staff. Major credit cards.

Toula's Taverna $$–$$$ *Agni; Tel. 0663 91350.* Open daily for lunch and dinner. The most recently established of Agni's remarkable triumvirate of tavernas, Toula's has also received rave reviews from the British broadsheets. A seafood meal here is likely to be a holiday highlight. Try the mussels *saganáki,* squid, lobster grilled sea bream, or the prawn pilaf. You can't go wrong no matter what you choose. Major credit cards.

Porto $$ *Harbor front, Kassiópi; Tel. 0663 81228.* Open daily noon–11pm. Excellent food in a traditional taverna setting with a lovely terrace shaded by an ancient giant plane tree. Interesting menu with several Greek and local specials. Prompt and friendly service. Major credit cards.

Tría Adélfia (Three Brothers) Taverna $$ *on the harbor in Kassiópi; Tel. 0663 81211.* Open daily for lunch and dinner. Set on a large terrace overlooking the pretty harbor. The menu here is nothing special, but the quality of food is high, particularly the fresh fish caught by the owner. Major credit cards.

Taverna Istoni $ *Main Street, Kassiópi; Tel. 0663 81032.* Open daily all day. A modern take on the simple Greek taverna, with lots of home-made Corfiote dishes as well as food for homesick Brits, including excellent-value English breakfasts. Cash only.

Taverna Kouloúra $$ *Kouloúra; Tel. 0663 91253.* Open daily all day. Simple, quiet, friendly fish taverna with an unbeatable location overlooking one of Corfu's most photographed harbors. Choose your dish from the cold display. Major credit cards.

Corfu

Spiros (Kati Thavres Taverna) $–$$ *Kamináki; Tel. 0663 91211.* Open daily all day. Typically charming family-owned taverna right on the beach of this picturesque little village. Ignore the menu and go for the blackboard specials; fresh fish is a specialty. Drivers should be cautious on the steep hill down to Kamináki. Cash only.

The West

Lucciola Inn $$$ *Sgombou (main Paleokastrítsa–Corfu Town road); Tel. 0661 99224.* Open daily for lunch and dinner. On the way back from Paleokastrítsa, be sure to stop off at this lovely old house, which dates from 1897. You will be treading in famous footsteps, as many celebrities — including Alec Guinness, Vivien Leigh, the Durrells, and even "Zorba" himself (Anthony Quinn) — have eaten here. Relax in the lovely garden and order *spetzofaï* (sausages in pepper sauce), *frigadelli* (lamb's liver), or fish Spetses-style. On Saturday nights, proprietor Vangelis performs with his *bouzoúki* band. Major credit cards.

Chez George $$$ *Paleokastrítsa Beach; Tel. 0663 41233.* Open daily for lunch and dinner. One of the most reliable seafood restaurants in Paleokastrítsa, in a fine location at the edge of the beach. Major credit cards.

Paxos

La Rosa di Paxos $$–$$$ *on the harbor in Lákka; Tel. 0662 31471.* Open daily for lunch and dinner. This very pretty waterside restaurant is the perfect place to take in the harbor scenery and atmosphere of Paxos. Excellent international and Greek cuisine. Major credit cards.

INDEX

144